CRICUT

3 Books In 1 – The Ultimate Manual for Beginners to Master The Cricut Maker and Explore Air 2. Discover all the Projects Ideas You Can Create and How to Start a Profitable Cricut Business.

Pamela Craft

Copyright © 2021 Pamela Craft

All rights reserved.

TABLE OF CONTENTS

CRICUT MAKER FOR BEGINNERS

Introduction 20

    History of the Cricut Maker 21

CHAPTER 1: What Is Cricut? 23

    What Can Be Achieved with Cricut Maker? 25

    Realize Your First Project 26

    How to Set Up a Brand New Cricut Maker in Under an Hour 26

CHAPTER 2: Choosing the Right Cricut for You 29

    Model Overview 29

    Cricut Explore One 29

    Cricut Explore Air 30

    Cricut Explore Air 2 30

    Cricut Maker 31

    Choosing the Right Cricut for You 32

CHAPTER 3: What Can It Cut with Cricut Maker 35

    Materials You Can Cut Using the Cricut Maker 35

    Vinyl 36

    Paper 37

    Chipboard 38

Fabric 39

Felt 40

Cardstock 41

Fondant 42

CHAPTER 4: What You Can't Do with Cricut Maker 49

What You Can't do with the Cricut Maker 49

CHAPTER 5: Differences Between Cricut Maker and Cricut Explore Air 2 53

Commonalities 53

Differences 53

CHAPTER 6: Choose the Best Accessories for Cricut Maker 59

Weeder 59

Basic Tool Set 60

Brayer 61

Scoring Stylus 62

Portable Trimmer 63

Sewing Kit 64

Self-Healing Rotary Mat 64

True Control Knife 65

Best Cricut Ideas into Your Cricut Projects 65

CHAPTER 7: Craft Ideas for Your Cricut Machine 69

Custom Graphic T-shirts 69

Wall Decals 72

Make Stickers with Your Cricut 73

Making Planner Sticker 76

CHAPTER 8: Some Works You Can Do with Cricut Maker 79

Cricut Maker Projects 79

DIY Mini Felt Stocking Gift Card Holder 79

Charming Donut Reading Set 80

Entertaining Penguin Christmas card 81

Projects to Create Fabric Cuts Thanks To Cricut Maker 82

Texture Projects to Try with your Cricut Maker 83

1. Blankets 83

2. Felt Dolls and Soft Toys 83

3. Infant Clothes 83

4. Doll Clothes 84

5. Texture Christmas Projects (Ornaments and Christmas Stockings) 84

6. Texture Appliques 84

7. Texture Key rings 84

8. Texture Coasters 84

9. Stick Cushions 85

10. Pads and Cushions 85

11. Children Clothes 85

12. A Sewing Organizer for your Cricut Maker 85

13. A Kids Backpack 85

14. Producer Dust Cover 85

CHAPTER 9: How You Can Monetize FROM Your Creations 87

How to Make Money with Cricut 87

How Do You Know When It's Time to Start a Shop? 88

Should I Quit My Day Job and Go All In? 88

How Can I Make Sure People Will Buy My Products? 88

Do I Need to Make Enough of Each Item in My Shop to Keep and Inventory? 89

Do I Need to Create a Shop in Order to Make Money with Cricut? 89

How Should I Price My Items? 90

What are the Best Platforms on Which to sell my Crafts? 91

What Kinds of Things Can I Make with Cricut to Make Money? 92

3D Puzzles 92

3D Wall Art 92

Aprons 92

CHAPTER 10: Cricut Machine Maintenance & Troubleshooting 93

Blade Life 93

Replacing the Cutting Blade 93

Replacing the Cutting Mat 94

Cleaning and Greasing Your Cricut Machine 94

Machine Dial Not Working 95

Machine Tearing or Dragging Materials 96

Machine Not Cutting Through Material 97

CHAPTER 11: Cricut Tips, Tricks, and Hacks 99

Careful Peeling 99

Careful Vinyl Storage 99

Keep Your Blade Sharp 100

Organize Your Cricket Blades 100

Easy Cleaning 100

Use Any Pen Brand You Want 100

The Vinyl Weeding Hack 101

Find Software Freebies 101

Store Supplies on a Pegboard 101

Easy Mat Cleaning 101

Vinyl Hack #2: Slap Bracelets 102

Wood Bin Material Organization 102

Cut Materials with Straight Edges 102

Use Free Digital Resources 102

Fix Materials with Painter's Tape 102

Use Transfer Tape for Neat Curved Surfaces 103

Write Down Your Cheats 103

Use Magazine Holders 104

Use Adhesives on Wood 104

Check Design Space for Freebies First 104

Conclusion 105

CRICUT PROJECT IDEAS

Introduction 110

CHAPTER 1: Why Should You Start Using A Cricut Machine? 113

Cricut as a Hobby 116

CHAPTER 2: Make Money with Cricut Machine 119

Selling for Profit 119

Vinyl Crafts are the Most Lucrative 120

Wall Art 120

Custom Decals 120

Children Related Wall Decals 120

The Wedding Industry is Alive and Well 120

Cricut Cake Toppers 121

Leather Earrings 121

Time Management 122

Productivity 122

Great Cricut Ideas to Bring in Some Cash 123

CHAPTER 3: Is It Possible to Build a Business with the Cricut Machine? How? 125

- Setting Up Your Cricut Business 125
- Setting Up a Website 125
- Advertising 126
- Taking Orders and Shipping 127

CHAPTER 4: Beginner Projects with the Cricut Explore Air 2 129

- How to Make Simple Handmade Cards 129
- Simple T-Shirt 131
- Basswood Quote with Vinyl Highlights 133
- A Flower Corsage 135

CHAPTER 5: Beginner Projects with Cricut Maker 137

- Shamrock Earrings 137
- Valentine's Day Classroom Cards 139
- Cricut Burlap Wreaths 140
- Personalized Pillows 142
- Cards! 143
- Printable Stickers 143

CHAPTER 6: Advanced Projects with the Cricut Explore Air 2 145

- How to Make a Leather Bracelet 145
- Making a Stencil for Painting with the Cricut Explore Air 2 146
- Making a Vinyl Sticker 146

Giant Vinyl Stencils 147

Cricut Quilts 148

Cricut Unicorn Backpack 148

Diamond Planters 151

CHAPTER 7: Advanced Projects with the Cricut Maker 155

A Large 3D Cricut Shadowbox 155

Engraved Jewelry with Cricut 157

Cricut 3D Decorations 159

CHAPTER 8: Project and Ideas with Vynil 163

Texture Cuts 163

Balsa Wood Cuts 163

Thick Leather Cuts 163

Custom made Cards 163

Jigsaw Puzzles 164

Christmas Tree Ornaments 164

Blankets 164

Felt Dolls and Soft Toys 164

Shirt Transfers 164

Doll Clothes 165

Texture Appliques 165

Calligraphy Signs 165

Gems Making 165

Wedding Invitations and Save the Dates 166

Wedding Menus, Place Cards, and Favor Tags 166

Shading Book 166

Napkins 166

Texture Key rings 167

Headbands and Hair Decorations 167

Cake Toppers 167

Refrigerator Magnets 167

Window Decals 167

Scrapbooking Embellishments 168

Art Foam Cuts 168

Boxes and 3D Shapes 168

Stencils 168

Transitory Tattoos 168

Washi Tape 169

Tended to Envelopes 169

Dish sets Decals 169

Adornments 169

Pad Transfers 170

3D Bouquet 170

Present Tags 170

CHAPTER 9: Project and Ideas with Paper 171

Recipe Stickers 171

Wedding Invitations 173

Custom Notebooks 175

Paper Flowers 176

CHAPTER 10: Projects and Ideas with Glass 179

Etched Monogrammed Glass 179

Live, Love, Laugh Glass Block 180

Unicorn Wine Glass 181

CHAPTER 11: Projects and Ideas with Clothing 183

Easy Lacey Dress 183

Dinosaur T-Shirt 184

Flower Garden Tote Bag 185

CHAPTER 12: Projects and Ideas with Fabric 187

Tassels 187

Monogrammed Drawstring Bag 188

Paw Print Socks 189

Night Sky Pillow 190

Conclusion 193

CRICUT EXPLORE AIR 2 FOR BEGINNERS

Introduction 196

CHAPTER 1: How to Use the Cricut Explore Air 2 199

    Setting Up the Cricut Explore Air 2 200

    What's in the Box 200

    Major Features 201

    Why Choose Cricut Explore Air 2 202

    What Do You Need to Succeed? 202

    Controls 202

    Tip 203

    Let's Start 203

    Cricut Explore Air 2: Recommended Configuration 204

    How Do You Use Layer Technology? 204

    How Do You Overlay Your Iron Designs? 204

    What Kind of Iron Can Be Used When Stacking? 205

    Realizing Your First Project 206

    Cutting Letters and Shapes for Scrapbooking 206

    Cutting Letters 207

CHAPTER 2: What It Can Cut with Cricut Explore Air 2 209

CHAPTER 3: Differences Between Cricut Maker and Cricut Explore Air 2 213

    Model Overview: Maker vs. Air 2 213

Versatility 213

Cutting Specifications 214

Price 215

Longevity 215

Software 216

Sewing projects 216

Portability 216

Easy to Use 217

Cartridges 217

Print and Then Cut 218

General Verdict 218

CHAPTER 4: Choose the Best Accessories for Cricut Explore Air 2 219

Cricut Tools and Accessory 219

Cricut Explore Cutting Blades 219

Cutting Mats 220

The Circuit Weeder 220

The Cricut Scraper 220

The Cricut Spatula 221

The Cricut Tweezers 221

The Cricut Scissors 221

The Cricut Scoring Tool 221

The Cricut Easy Press 222

The Cricut Brightpad 222

The Cricut Cuttlebug Machine 222

Cricut Mats 223

How to Make Your Cutting Mat Sticky Again 225

General Maintenance 226

CHAPTER 5: Craft Ideas for Your Cricut Cutting Machine 227

DIYs with Cricut Machine 227

Infusible Ink T-Shirt 227

Handmade Paper Flower Corsage 229

Coffee Mug 231

Fairy House Card 232

Birthday Garland Banner 235

Advent Calendar 236

CHAPTER 6: Some Works You Can Do with Cricut Explore Air 2 ... 239

Simple Projects to Start With 239

Custom Graphic T-shirt 239

Stickers with Your Cricut 242

False Cowhide Home Keychain 244

Calfskin Hair Bow 246

Fun Foam Stamps 247

CHAPTER 7: How You Can Monetize from Your Creations 249

- Making Money with Cricut 249
- 50+ Business Ideas You Can Make with Your Cricut and Sell 250
- Ideas for Selling Your Cricut Crafts 252
- Online Marketplaces for Selling Crafts 253
- Etsy 254
- Artesanum 254
- Lulishop 255
- Coolmaison 255
- Unique Species 256

CHAPTER 8: Frequently Asked Questions 257

- Why is My Material Tearing? 257
- Do I Need to Convert My Image to an SVG? 257
- Where Can I Buy Materials? 257
- Do I Need a Printer to Use My Cricut? 258
- Where Can I Get Compatible Images? 258
- Where Can I Get Compatible Fonts? 258
- Why is My Blade Cutting All the Way through My Material? 258
- Do I Need to Be Connected to the Internet to Use Design Space? 259
- Which Operating Systems Are Compatible with Design Space? 259
- Can I Use Design Space on My Chromebook? 259

Can I Use Design Space on Multiple Devices I Own? 259

Is There a Time Limit on Using Images I've Purchased through Design Space? 260

How Can I Unweld an Image in Design Space? 260

How Do I Set Design Space to Operate on the Metric System? 260

What Types of Images Can I Upload through Cricut's Design Space iOS or Android Apps? 260

Using Move and Hide, Can I Move Printable Images to Another Mat? 261

In Move and Hide, Is it Possible to Move Multiple Images to a New Mat All at Once? 261

How Many Images Can I Move to One Mat? 261

Can I Save Money by Hiding Images from the Mat? 261

Can I Save the Layout of My Mat? 261

Is Cricut Design Space Compatible with My Version of Internet Explorer? 262

What Features Are Available on Which Apps? 262

CHAPTER 9: Tips & Strategies for the First Project 265

Setting the Machine 265

Cartridges and Keypad 266

How to detach your cut from the cutting mat? 269

CHAPTER 10: Cricut Explore Air 2 Project Ideas with Vinyl 271

Personalized Mugs (Iron-On Vinyl) 272

Personalized Coaster Tiles 274

Vinyl Chalkboard 276

Vinyl Herringbone Bracelet 278

Cloud Vinyl Wallpaper 279

Printable Vinyl Easter Eggs... 280

Game over Tablet Vinyl 282

Conclusion 283

CRICUT MAKER FOR BEGINNERS

A comprehensive guide for beginners to mastering your cricut maker and designing amazing projects

Pamela Craft

INTRODUCTION

The Cricut Maker is basically a 3D printer in your hands. You can design and print whatever you want, any time you want. The Cricut Maker is a great tool for anyone who wants to create their own custom design on a computer, like scrapbookers or crafters. The Cricut Maker is a machine that cuts fabric without using any blades. It is a great option for anyone looking to cut their own fabric.

Amazon has started selling the Cricut Maker, which is designed for cutting out vinyl for scrapbooking and crafts. The device allows you to create designs on a vinyl stencil with an included stylus. The Cricut Maker is a wonderful gift for any crafter who wants to get into cutting images or vinyl. The machine cuts and engraves all kinds of materials, including paper, vinyl, fabric, and more. The Cricut maker is a cutting machine that allows you to create your own designs on fabric. You can make and cut any shape from fabric. This machine is able to cut through the vinyl, iron on transfers, and fleece.

If you own a Cricut, get the new Cricut Maker. It's a $149 cutting machine that can cut thin vinyl and paper. The Cricut Maker is a tool that allows you to cut and design vinyl or paper quickly. It cuts directly on the vinyl or paper, so you won't have to worry about damaging your work space. The Cricut maker is a cutting machine that allows you to create decorative papercraft projects. The cutting machine cuts vinyl and sticker images into any shape.

The Cricut Maker is a sewing and crafting device designed by Provo Craft. It's comparable to other popular brands of fabric cutters, including the Sizzix 12″ Vagabond, the Sizzix Big Shot Plus, etc. The Cricut Maker is versatile and can be used for cutting, lettering and embossing.

The Cricut Maker is an exciting piece of equipment with many capabilities. It's easy to use and has plenty of potential for fun projects. There are multiple ways to make things with the Cricut Maker, including using pre-made designs from the online store or creating your own (starting from scratch) using Cricut Design Space software.

History of the Cricut Maker

The Cricut Maker is an electronic cutting machine produced by Provo Craft. It is a small device that can be used to cut a variety of materials, such as paper and cardstock, fabric, and vinyl. It was released in September 2017.

In December 2016, American multinational office supply company, Staples Inc., announced that it would carry the product in all of its US retail stores, which sold products for crafts and hobbies. Staples opened pre-orders for the Cricut Maker on their website from January 26 to February 7 and began selling it on the online site from March 13 through April 10 to allow customers to try out the new product before purchasing it at their local store. The Cricut Maker was first sold officially at Staples retail stores beginning April 13 for US$250. On May 18, 2017, both Amazon Canada and Amazon UK started selling Cricut Makers with delivery scheduled for June 1, 2017. Both markets only stocked the Graphite color option of the device. Also in late May 2017, news came that Target stores were considering selling the device later in 2017. Staples started selling the Cricut Maker in Canada starting June 26, 2017. In June 2017, both Amazon UK and Canadian news outlets announced that Cricut Canada was planning on releasing the device on July 1, 2017. At an event in Canada, Staples had announced that they would also be selling the machine starting August 1. Staples has confirmed that it plans to continue selling the Cricut Maker in its stores, as well as online. The company says that it will sell each of these machines for $249.99 CAD or $199 USD for those who have a Canadian credit card (similar to what was done for the Stampin' Up! Big Shot and the Craftsmart 3), but that shipping would vary based on location. Additionally, Staples will also offer a 30-day money-back guarantee if customers are not satisfied with their purchase.

Due to high demand in Canada, some consumers have reported having difficulties buying a machine due to online preorder availability running out before shipping began. Cricut Canada responded to this with a statement on Facebook, saying that shipments were limited to 5000 units and that the majority of those who had preordered a machine would be receiving their purchase in September 2017. The company also stated that more units would become available as of October 2017.

The Cricut Maker is priced at £199.99 in the United Kingdom.

On December 11, 2017, Staples Canada announced an end to sales of the Cricut Maker effective immediately due to lack of support from Cricut. On November 23, 2018, an additional inventory of the Cricut Maker was found by a Staples employee and listed on an eBay store. This stock was purchased and shipped to a Canadian company that was called to request it. The use of the Cricut Maker is not prohibited by the courts even though its manufacturer filed bankruptcy in October 2018.

The Cricut Maker was first released in September 2017, sold exclusively at Staples retail stores. It is also available on Amazon.com and Amazon.ca in the US and Canada, respectively; Europe-wide, including the UK and Europe, through SCALA; Australia through Craftworld; New Zealand; as well as Canada. Staples also offers it through its website. On March 21, 2018, it was announced that Cricut would supply its hardware to Cuttlebug, which will then be available to purchase on their website in the United States and Germany later that month.

The price of this unit is $249.99 USD when purchased from the American Staples company store. However, if one registers their machine within 30 days of purchasing it at Staples or anywhere else that sells them for $249.

CHAPTER 1: WHAT IS CRICUT?

Maybe you obtained a Cricut gadget for Christmas or a birthday, yet it's nonetheless sitting in its box. Or perhaps you're an avid crafter searching out an easy device to make crafting easier. Or perhaps you've visible heaps of cool challenge photographs on Pinterest and wondered "How the heck do they reduce the ones elaborate designs? I want to try this!" or perhaps you've heard of Cricut. However, you're asking, "What is a Cricut gadget, and what are you able to do with it?" Well, you're inside the proper region; these days I'm going to introduce you to the Cricut Explore Air gadget and inform you approximately all of the cool matters it may do!

There aren't any extra cartridges; the entirety is performed digitally, so you can use any font or form that's in your laptop. And most of the Cricut machines paintings over Wi-Fi or Bluetooth, so that you can layout out of your iPhone or iPad, in addition to out of your laptop! The Cricut machines are smooth to apply, completely versatile, and best confined through your personal creativity!

What Is A Cricut Machine?
The Cricut is a die-reducing gadget (aka craft plotter or reducing gadget). You can consider it like a printer; you create a photograph or layout in your laptop and then send it to the gadget. Except that in place of printing your layout, the Cricut gadget cuts it out of something fabric you need! The Cricut Explore Air can reduce paper, vinyl, fabric, craft foam, decal paper, fake leather-based, and extra!
In fact, in case you need to apply a Cricut like a printer, it may try this too! There is an accent slot with the inside of the gadget and you may load a marker in there after the Cricut "draw" your layout for you. It's ideal for purchasing a terrific handwritten appearance in case your handwriting isn't all that great. The Explore collection of Cricut machines lets you get admission to a big virtual library of "cartridges" in place of the use of bodily cartridges, as I did in college.

With this approach, you may use Cricut Design Space (there on line layout software) to take any textual content or form from the library and ship it for your Cricut to be reduced out. You may even add your personal designs in case you need to!

With a Cricut gadget, the opportunities are endless! All you want is a Cricut gadget, Design Space, something to reduce, and your personal creativity!

What is a Cricut Maker

The Cricut Maker is a new "3D" cutting tool by Cricut. The machine can create projects, including signs, picture frames, and more. It does not require a computer or tablet for use. The Cricut Maker is the first machine of its kind to be sold without requiring any design software in order to make projects. Instead, you can upload images to the Cricut Maker using your phone's camera or a USB drive.

The Cricut Maker uses "Cricut Expression" cartridges for the creation of projects. These cartridges can be either purchased from Cricut or created yourself using a computer and design software such as Tinkercad. The machine is capable of making projects up to 12 inches in size and comes with an array of tools to help you create your projects more easily. These tools include a cutting wheel, ruler, and spatula. The Cricut Maker is able to cut up to two layers of cardstock material at once or can cut one layer with multiple passes through the machine. There are also several color options available for the Maker, including black, red, white and teal blue.

Cricut announced it was planning on creating a new 3D machine in March 2017 after releasing its Create 3D printer in 2016. It was then officially announced on July 17, 2017, that the product would be called "Cricut Maker" and would cost $1,000 USD less than their competitor's product (the XYZprinting da Vinci). Cricut announced the product at the 2017 International Consumer Electronics Show in Las Vegas.

What Can Be Achieved with Cricut Maker?

There are TONS of factors you may do with a Cricut gadget! There's no manner I should even list all of the opportunities, however right here are some famous varieties of tasks to offer you a concept of what the gadget can do.

- Cut out amusing shapes and letters for scrapbooking
- Make custom, homemade cards for any unique occasion
- An onesie or a t-shirt
- Make a leather-based bracelet
- Make buntings and different birthday celebration decorations
- Create your personal stencils for painting
- Make a vinyl decal to your vehicle window
- Label stuff on your pantry or in a playroom
- Make monogram pillows
- Create your personal Christmas ornaments
- Address an envelope
- Decorate a mug, cup, or tumbler
- Etch glass at home
- Create your personal wall decals
- Make a painted wood sign
- Make your personal window clings
- Cut appliqués or duvet squares
- Create decals for a stand mixer

...and heaps of different tasks that are too severe to list!

Here are the Cricut machines I mentioned in this text; click on the photographs beneath to discover extra approximately every gadget. And in case you're searching to shop for a great crafting device, I noticeably propose the Cricut Explore machines! I use mine quite an awful lot each day, and it rocks!

Realize Your First Project

Have a modern-day Cricut Maker, however, are you sitting on the container? This grade by grade academic and video indicates the way to get set up and walks you all of the manner thru finishing your first assignment!

Having a modern-day Cricut system may be a bit daunting; they're so effective, and there are such a lot of opportunities for the use of them. But don't worry, they aren't truly complex or difficult to use! I'm going to stroll you thru the setup method for a modern-day Cricut Maker system, grade by grade: from pulling it out of the container and plugging it into your laptop all the way thru finishing your first actual assignment! (And in case you don't have a Maker, I'm running on setup tutorials for the alternative machines and could submit the ones ASAP, however with inside the intervening time, the stairs are quite comparable so that you need to be capable of complying with together with this academic!)

For the ones of you who're simply getting began out, I even have an entire manual to the accessories & components that each Cricut newbie needs (and which of them are simply "nice-to-have" that you could splurge on later in case you want). And in case you're nevertheless at the fence or nevertheless have questions on the Maker, test out my post answering all of the not unusual place questions on the Maker!

How to Set Up a Brand New Cricut Maker in Under an Hour

- Time spent doing stuff: forty minutes
- Time spent ready around: 15 minutes
- Total assignment time: fifty-five minutes

Tools

- Cricut Maker
- USB cable (covered inside the container with the Maker)

- Power cord (covered inside the container with the Maker)
- Rotary Blade + Drive Housing (covered inside the container with the Maker)
- Fine Point Blade + Housing (covered inside the container with the Maker)
- Fine Point Pen (covered inside the container with the Maker)
- Fabric Grip Mat 12"x12" (covered inside the container with the Maker)
- Light Grip Mat 12"x12" (covered inside the container with the Maker)
- laptop, tablet, or cell tool this is related to the internet

Materials

The packet of first assignment substances that got here together, along with your Maker (or portions of cardstock and a small scrap of fabric)

Instructions

Cricut has lately modified their new system setup academic, and it does not consist of a complete preliminary assignment. I'm running to get a brand new video filmed to stroll you thru the brand new setup academic, however with inside the intervening time the primary steps to get the system truly related for your laptop and registered are nevertheless the same, it's simply the whole thing after that element that has modified And don't overlook to test out my other Cricut tutorials and assignment ideas!

I desire this lets you get began out together along with your Cricut! If you're modern-day to Cricut, test out a number of my newbie tutorials:

It's a lot laugh making Cricut Projects. You can create all types of crafts together along with your Cricut Explore or Cricut Maker reducing machine. There are many excellent Cricut thoughts to try. Here you may discover a developing listing of undertaking tutorials, Cricut information, recommendations, critiques and resources. Whether you're new to Cricut or a long term Cricut user, I hope you discover something you enjoy.

CHAPTER 2: CHOOSING THE RIGHT CRICUT FOR YOU

Model Overview

Purchasing a Cricut Machine may not be very cheap, but choosing your model should mostly depend on your needs and what you wish to do with these machines. If you have never used a Cricut machine before, then you will need to start with the easiest machine to operate. As a manufacturer of tools and accessories for DIY crafts, Cricut has several models that can serve all kinds of users. From all the Cricut Models, there are four which are most interesting: the ones from the Explore family (Cricut Explore One, Cricut Explore Air, and Cricut Explore Air 2), and of course, the Cricut Maker, which is the best Cricut Machine you can hope for. Before you even start to think about the price of these models, it would be nice to understand what they can do.

Cricut Explore One

This machine is the most basic one you can get from the Explore family. Derived from its predecessor (Cricut Explore), this tool can be the perfect starter machine for you if you are not familiar with any of the Cricut products. Like most of the Cricut products, it's compatible with Design Space software (and allows you to upload your own images free of charge), can work with Cricut Cartridges, or can cut a pretty wide variety of materials. Plus, it comes with Smart Set Dial, a function you can use to easily configure the settings for each material.

If you just want to start your own small business and have something pretty interesting in mind, but you don't want to invest too much, for now, the Cricut Explore One can be the perfect choice for you. It can be bought for less than $200 on the Cricut website, Amazon, or other retailers.

When you have great project ideas, then the sky is the limit when it comes to how much money you can make from your Cricut projects, so spending this amount can be considered a minor and very profitable investment on your part.

Cricut Explore Air

If you are looking for an amazing DIY value, look no further, as the Cricut Explore Air can be the perfect choice for you. In terms of features, this version is a bit more advanced than the original Cricut Explore. It includes the Smart Set Dial, a double tool holder for writing and one-click cutting, and it works with Design Space software (for Mac/iOS/Windows/Android). Obviously, you will be able to upload your own images free of charge, but the machine can also work with Cricut Cartridges and cut plenty of materials. When it comes to connectivity, Cricut Explore Air comes with a Bluetooth option for wireless cutting. This type of connectivity can be very handy in plenty of cases but bear in mind that it might fail if the projects you are trying to create are quite big.

The manufacturer, Amazon, or other retailers can offer great deals on this machine, so don't be shocked if you can find this product at a heavily discounted price. When you think of what it can do, it's definitely worth it to pay a discounted price for Cricut Explore Air.

Cricut Explore Air 2

If you are looking for the best product from the Explore Family, then you will need to try Cricut Explore Air 2. This machine is like an upgraded version of Explore Air, and it's known for its time-saving performance. It has more features than the older versions, and so far, it's been a very appreciated product by plenty of users. The biggest advantage of this version is that it comes with both a Smart Set dial and Fast Mode. So you can easily go through material settings, plus you write and cut 2 times faster, hence its time-saving performance and increased productivity.

Plus, you will get all the existing features of the Explore Family products like:

- Bluetooth connectivity for wireless cutting
- Double tool holding for both writing and one-click cutting
- It allows you to upload your own images using the Design Space software
- It can cut plenty of materials
- It can work with Cricut Cartridges

Therefore, if you are looking for a powerful Cricut Machine that has plenty of features and can be a time-saver, then the Cricut Explore Air 2 is the perfect choice for you. When it comes to the price, this version is a bit more expensive compared to the older versions, but it totally worth the investment, especially when you buy this product at a discounted price or with a bundle (this option may include different accessories).

Cricut Maker

Without any doubt, the premium or the flagship machine of Cricut is the Maker. If you are looking to expand your craft business, then this is the right tool for you. The Cricut Maker has plenty of features, as you can see below:

- It has Bluetooth connectivity included, for wireless cutting
- It comes with a double tool holder for writing and one-click cutting
- It allows you to upload your images for free using the Design Space software
- You can cut even more materials compared to the older versions
- It comes with Fast Mode included, so you can write or cut two times faster
- It has a special Rotary Blade for fabrics
- It includes a Knife Blade for thicker materials
- Simple and Double Scoring Wheel
- Adaptive Tool System, which is a feature for cutting hundreds of other materials

One of the best things with the Cricut machines is that you can select the color that you like the most, so it's not like you are limited to one color (white or black). Therefore, for the Explore version, you can select between Green and Wild Orchid. The Explore One comes with more color options: Blue, Pink Poppy, Navy Bloom, Coral, or Grey. You will get different color options with Explore Air: Gold, Teal, Wild Orchid, Poppy, and Blue. By far, the Explore Air 2 has the most options you can select from, including White Pearl (Martha Stewart), Wisteria, Sunflower, Sky, Rose, Raspberry, Persimmon, Periwinkle, Peacock, Mint, Merlot, Lilac, Gold, Ivory (Anna Griffin), Fuschi, Denim, Coral, Cobalt, Cherry Blossom, Boysenberry, Blue, and Black.

The Cricut Maker only comes with three color options: Rose, Blue, and Champagne. Some colors may be exclusive to specific retailers, so these colors may not be found in the manufacturer's online store.

Choosing the Right Cricut for You

There are several aspects you will need to consider when selecting the right Cricut Machine for you, like:

• Your experience with these kinds of machines
• Your budget
• What projects you want to create
• What materials you want to cut

When you don't have too much experience with such machines, and you are definitely not familiar with any of the Cricut Machines, then it's wise to choose an entry-level machine from the Explore family. Perhaps this is why they included these machines in the Explore family, as it lets you explore the functions and features of a Cricut Machine. Any of these machines can be considered teasers of the Cricut Maker, which can be easily considered the ultimate cutting machine.

If you are a beginner but want to quickly learn and implement some of your great ideas into projects, then the Cricut Explore Air 2 can be considered the perfect option for you. You can easily find a color you prefer, plus you will find all kinds of deals from the Cricut Shop or online retailers, offering you the product at a good price.

However, if you are very familiar with these machines, and you want to cut even thicker materials, then you really need to get the Cricut Maker, especially if you have some projects in mind that can help you make plenty of money. Regardless of the version you select, in most cases the prices are reasonable, and you can easily recover your initial investment in such a machine.

CHAPTER 3: WHAT CAN IT CUT WITH CRICUT MAKER

Materials You Can Cut Using the Cricut Maker

There are many different materials that the machines can use for any project you desire, and we will be breaking down which machine can use what materials. Something that you should know is that there are materials that the Maker can cut and the other machines cannot, as a matter of fact, they include over one hundred different types of fabric.

The official website of the Cricut machines periodically upgrades, in what they say the machines can cut, so as a result, you will need to check their website often. In doing so, you will realize what you can still cut, even if it may have been taken off the list.

We will go over a variety of them in detail to get a better understanding of how truly remarkable the Cricut machine really is! Get inspired by a collection of diverse, high-quality materials, all designed to cut perfectly with Cricut machines. Material finishes ranging from fun and flashy to polished and rich. These materials make it easy to achieve the exact look you want.

Once you get more comfortable using the different types of materials, you will easily be able to create projects that have multiple materials in one. Utilize resources such as this book to refer to when you have questions relating to what type of material to use and when. The more you know, the better your project will be!

Vinyl

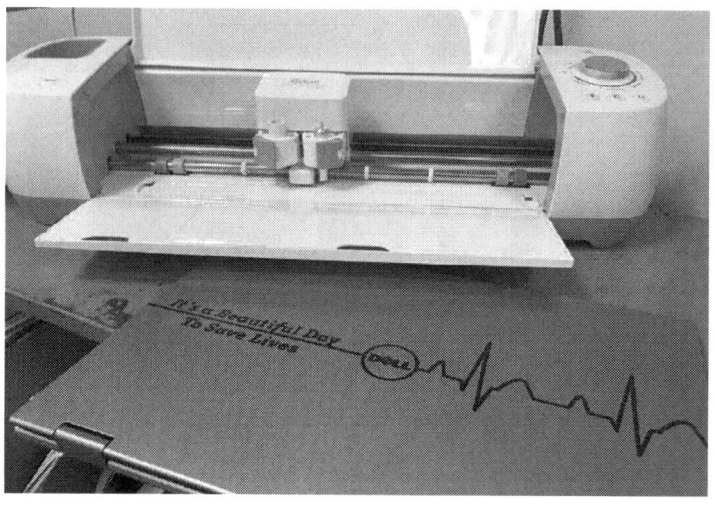

Adhesive vinyl for Cricut cutting machines come in a wide variety of colors, designs, and uses. The adhesive properties can either be semi-permanent (easily removable with adhesive remover) or permanent. Semi-permanent is typically used for indoor projects, such as wall decals or window clings. Permanent vinyl would be used for outdoor use, such as holiday decor and tabletop designs. Those are perfect for making stickers, indoor and outdoor items, and even 'printing' on mugs and T-shirts. Once you get into it, it is truly addictive to acquire different colors and types. For example, you can get chalkboard vinyl, which is awesome for labeling, or outdoor vinyl, which will look great on your car window. These materials can be purchased at virtually any craft shop, and they are not too expensive if you do a little canvassing. Double check that it is indeed the type of vinyl you are looking for. Vinyl is the most used material for Cricut projects outside of paper because it is one of the most versatile materials to work with. Adhesive vinyl is a great starting point for creators who are new to Cricut but want to branch outside of paper crafting. Adhesive vinyl is a material that will need to be weeded, as designs are typically cut out of the vinyl, and the negative space will need to be removed in order to see the design.

Paper

There is a wide variety of paper products that can be cut using the Cricut machine. Some varieties include cardstock, which is one of the most popular; corrugated cardboard; foil embossed; Kraft board; scrapbooking paper; pearl; sparkle/shimmer; and poster board. Paper products can come in a wide range of sizes, with 12'x12' being the most common and easily applied type as it fits perfectly on a 12'x12' cutting mat. Paper is most commonly used in card projects, but it can also assist in wall decor, gift boxes, cake toppers and lantern projects. Most crafters familiar with the Cricut recommend starting with the paper project first to get a handle on the different options that Cricut cutters have. Paper allows you to create intricate designs and get familiar with the cutting blade depth at the same time. What you should remember is that you need something to practice on, and a cheap printer paper works wonderfully for that. You will not feel bad for making mistakes because the material does not cost much. If you are feeling more creative than usual, you may get the colored paper too. This way, when you get the hang of cutting, you can create letters for cars or stencils. The following materials can only be used with the Cricut Maker machine.

Chipboard

The Cricut website sells a variety pack of this type of material, which is great for getting to know the material and what projects to use it for effectively. It is suggested to be used on projects such as sturdy wall art, school projects, photo frames and more. Since this material has a 1.5mm thickness, it can only be cut using the Cricut Knife blade. Chipboard is great for any type of project that requires dimensions, such as gingerbread or a haunted house around the holidays!

Fabric

The fabric is great if you have the Cricut Maker. Chances are that you will want to cut some textile with this machine on hand; that is why you should stock up on that and get extra just in case. You can obtain some cheap, scrappy fabrics to practice on before moving on to the proper fabrics for the projects.

This simple, yet classic material, is another favorite among Cricut Maker users. Many use fabrics to create custom clothing, home decor, and wall art. Imagine all the times you went out looking for the perfect top or skirt only to come back home empty-handed after many hours of searching. It would be ideal to find exactly what you want when you want it! Now, without the help of a bulky and outdated sewing machine, you can make simple and affordable clothing exactly the look and feel you want! Fabric is also a great material to make homemade gifts for friends and family. Lots of people enjoy curling up on the couch during the winter months, with a cozy quilt and a favorite movie.

Felt

Blended fibers between natural and synthetic are also common among craft felts. Felt is commonly used to help young children distinguish among different types of textiles. Felt is also commonly used in craft projects for all ages. The felt is easily cut with your Cricut Machine; no Deep Cut blade required! Felt can be used for: fun decor, kid's crafts, baby toys, stuffed shapes and more! When starting out on the Cricut Maker, this is one of the best materials to start out with. This material is very forgiving and will allow you to keep the gift-giving spirit going! This material is also great for creating faux flowers. You can bring the outside indoors, without maintenance or worrying about children or pets getting into a mess!

Cardstock

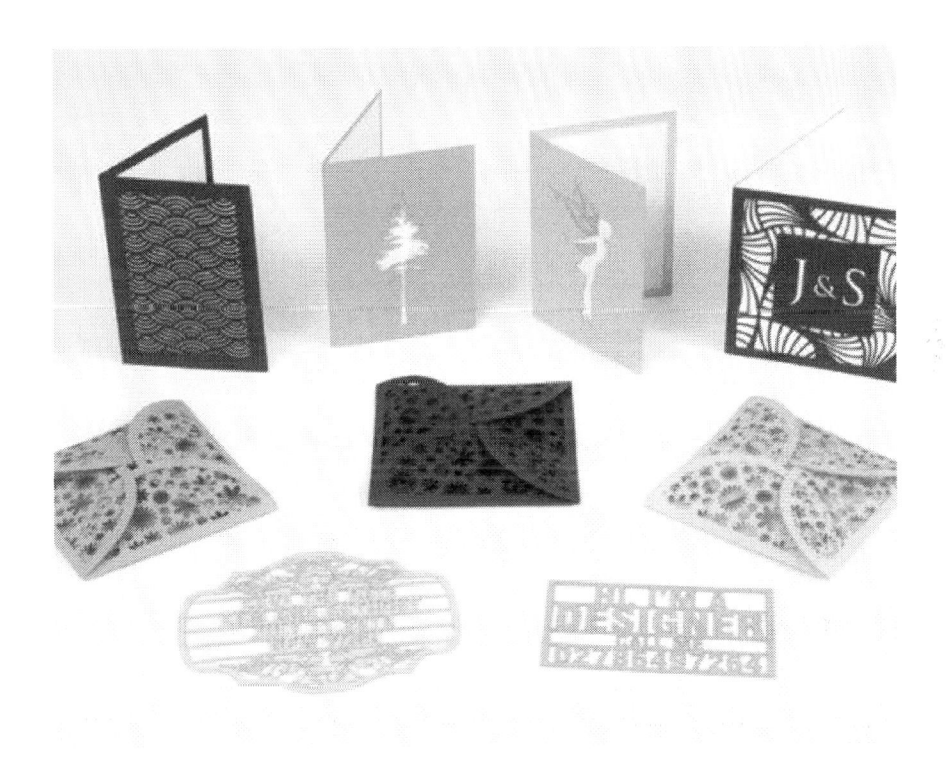

If you plan on making cards or labels, cardstock is a must. The more, the better. It is really awesome to have a large pile of it and just be able to cut to your heart's content. It will also help to practice once you have perfected cutting normal printing paper.

Fondant

Fondant is for those bakers out there. There is a possibility that you already have extra fondant lazing about in your home. However, it never hurts to have more. The awesome thing about fondant is that you can reuse it to an extent, depending on how well it freezes or how big the need is to freeze it before cutting. Of course, it is useful to have back up materials for the days that you are in a crafty sort of mood. Most materials are available on the Cricut website, so you can order them along with your Cricut machine. Everything will be delivered at once, and you will not have to buy anything again for a while.

It also depends on what sort of material you will be interested in for creating something awesome. If you are going to cut wood, for instance, you will have to stock up on that as you will be going through it quite fast if you are an enthusiastic and excitable crafter.

The Explore series can only cut certain items, and we are going to list them now.

- Tattoo paper
- Washi tape
- Paint chips
- Wax paper
- Faux suede
- Wrapping paper
- Washi paper
- Poster board
- Parchment paper
- Sticker paper
- Construction paper
- Photo paper
- Printable fabric
- Magnetic sheets
- Paper grocery bags
- Craft foam
- Window cling vinyl
- Cardstock
- Flannel
- Vellum
- Duck cloth
- Wool felt
- Corkboard
- Tissue paper
- Duct tape
- Matte vinyl
- Iron-on vinyl

- Leather up to 2.0 mm thick
- Sheet duct tape
- Oil cloth
- Soda cans
- Stencil film
- Glitter foam
- Metallic vellum
- Burlap
- Transparency film
- Chipboard that is up to 2.0 mm thick
- Aluminum metal that is up to .14 mm thick
- Stencil vinyl
- Glitter vinyl
- Glossy vinyl
- Faux leather up to 1.0 mm thick

Fabrics, when used with the Explore series, need to be stabilized with Heat N Bond. Examples of fabrics are shown on the list below:

- Denim
- Felt
- Silk
- Polyester

Other items that the Explore Series can cut are listed below:

- Chalkboard vinyl
- Adhesive vinyl
- Aluminum foil
- Cardboard

- Stencil film
- Dry erase vinyl
- Printable vinyl
- Outdoor vinyl
- Wood birch up to .5 mm thick
- Cardboard that is corrugated
- Shrink plastic
- Metallic vellum
- White core
- Rice paper
- Photo framing mat
- Pearl cardstock
- Cereal boxes
- Freezer paper
- Iron-on
- Printable iron-on
- Glitter iron-on
- Foil iron-on
- Foil embossed paper
- Neon iron-on
- Matte iron-on

The Maker can cut everything that the Explore series can cut, but it can cut so much more because the Explore series operates with three blades, but the Maker has six. The fact that it has six blades enables it to cut more, as well as thicker fabric. It also differs from the Explore series in the sense that the Maker does not have to use Heat N Bond to stabilize fabrics. This is a great thing because it means that you can go to a fabric store and choose a fabric and use it for a project with no preparation and no additional materials either.

The Maker is also able to utilize the rotary blade as well. This type of blade is new and it differs from the others that the Explore machines use because this blade spins and also twists with a gliding and rolling motion. This rolling action is going to allow the Maker to cut side to side, as well as up and down. Having a blade able to cut in any direction is going to help you with the ability to craft great projects. The Maker is even able to cut (up to) three layers of light cotton at the same time. This is great for projects that need uniform cuts.

The Maker is also able to use the knife blade, which is a more precise option and cuts better than the others before it. This blade can cut up to 2.4 mm thick fabric. This machine is also able to use ten times more power to cut than the others as well.

With that being said, the Maker can cut over a hundred different fabrics that others cannot. We will be listing some of those fabrics below:

- Waffle cloth
- Jacquard
- Gossamer
- Khaki
- Damask
- Faille
- Heather
- Lycra
- Mesh
- Calico
- Crepe paper
- Gauze
- Interlock knit
- Grocery bag

- Acetate
- Chantilly lace
- Boucle
- Corduroy
- EVA foam
- Tweed
- Tulle
- Moleskin
- Fleece
- Jersey
- Muslin
- Jute
- Terry cloth
- Velvet
- Knits
- Muslin

CHAPTER 4: WHAT YOU CAN'T DO WITH CRICUT MAKER

What You Can't do with the Cricut Maker

1. Cut any non - Delrin plastics with the Cricut Maker. Do NOT cut PET, PCV, PVC, LEXAN, ACETAL, Teflon (PTFE), any glass/crystal or other rigid plastic you may have.

2. From what I know you can't cut Nylon with the Cricut Maker... but have tried it anyway. Turns out it works for some plastics, but not others.

3. My local Cricut representatives tell me you can cut aluminum with the Cricut Maker as long as it's thin enough (less than .075").

4. I did a quick test of how well not-so-sturdy metals cut with the Cricut Maker... YMMV. I used 316 Stainless steel... Basically a very thick piece of steel, and it didn't cut too badly at all.

5. From what I can tell, the Cricut Maker will ONLY cut metal if it's thin enough (less than .075"). No matter how many times I tried to do a test cut on aluminum housing with the Cricut Maker, it would always end up cutting a chunk out of the aluminum housing and not allowing me to continue cutting.

6. "Some plastics" like Lucite or acrylic also seem to work OK with the Cricut Maker... but there are still materials that will not work...

7. Works fairly well with acrylic (skateboard decks, jigsaw puzzles, and other things I've done). But again, there are some materials that will not adhere to the Cricut Maker.

8. The Cricut Maker does not work for cutting any metal... "all-metal" as in cut through them or bend them too.... at least not to my knowledge.

9. The Cricut Maker will not cut paper with "all blade" settings, which leaves it pretty much limited to the "E" blade setting (see the top tip below for more info on this).

10. If you do manage to cut through metal with the Cricut Maker, you will probably have a VERY hard time cleaning the cut/chunk out of your plastic. The best bet is to get a cheater bar and a steel punch to tap out the chunk when you're done.

11. Just like the Silhouette, the Cricut Maker can cut through the vinyl, but you NEED A VERY GOOD PRESSURE SENSITIVE VINYL in order for it to work. If you're using something that doesn't adhere well and has an extremely high tack, it will not cut… believe me, I tried…

12. NEVER CUT ANYTHING THAT LOOKS LIKE IT MIGHT GET STUCK IN YOUR MACHINE! I've been told that if it does get stuck inside of the machine, you may end up breaking your machine trying to get your part out of the machine… So let common sense and wear protective gear when working with or around the Cricut Maker, especially when cutting metal.

13. The Cricut Maker will cut through most thin materials that aren't too thick, as long as they are clean and have NO HOLES OR EMPTY SPACE INSIDE THE SHAPE OF WHAT YOU'RE TRYING TO CUT!

14. Be careful not to cut the cord or power supply for the Cricut Maker….

15. The Cricut Maker requires the use of a blade tip that has teeth… much like a saw blade, in order to make a cut. I've been told that you can still use it without the teeth, but it will NOT make a cut…. I've also been told that you cannot do anything else with this machine if you remove the teeth from the blade tip….

16. According to all my tests, you can only use ONE BLADE AT A TIME. You cannot stack blade-tips on top of each other in an attempt to make your cuts thicker... It does not work...

17. From what I've figured out so far, there is only ONE WAY to align one piece of material against another piece of material so that both pieces are accurate and in alignment WHILE cutting ..... This is the most difficult part of the process, but once you figure this out, it goes surprisingly fast, and your cuts will look good and end up being accurate.... (you need this to cut delicate materials like vinyl or screen print etc., not sure about Delrin)

CHAPTER 5: DIFFERENCES BETWEEN CRICUT MAKER AND CRICUT EXPLORE AIR 2

The Cricut Maker and the Cricut Explore Air 2 are both cutting machines for crafting and card making, as well as similar designs with many interchangeable plastic parts. The differences between the two models will determine which model is best for you, your budget, and the workload you will place on your machine. Let's explore each of the models to see what they have in common and what sets them apart.

Commonalities

Both machines are manufactured by the same company, Provo Craft. The machines continue to evolve with new features being added, such as Bluetooth connectivity in addition to SD card support. Both models currently have a wireless Bluetooth feature that allows users to make designs from their smartphones or tablets. This allows for wireless use of the machine from afar; however, at this point, there are limited apps available for use, so you may not be able to create anything beyond greeting cards with this particular feature just yet. You can purchase blank cards that are compatible with both the maker and explore air 2 directly from Provo Craft or other retailers such as Hobby Lobby or Michael's crafts stores.

Differences

Design/Function: The Cricut Maker is a single-machine, while the Cricut Explore Air 2 has two devices that work together. The maker can be used as a stand-alone device for card and scrapbook printing. However, it is more frequently used in conjunction with the Explore Air 2 as they are designed to work together seamlessly from the start. The Cricut Maker has its own main power supply that will run both machines at once. One machine may need to be plugged in more frequently than the other depending on how frequently you will use your products; however, you can still run them simultaneously without using up too much power if needed.

Add-Ons: The Explore Air 2 includes additional stamp pad sets that allow you to create more stamps when compared to just using your mechanical cutting blades. You can turn a sheet of paper into a stencil with this machine over and over again until it becomes impossible for your artwork or designs to be seen.

The Cricut Maker only has the option for the stamp pad sets. The stamp pads can be purchased as individual colors and there is a little box on the front of your machine with several small holes that allow you to squeeze out the paint in a thin line to capture your design. This feature of this model is fairly simple but does allow for more versatility for different projects.

Price: The Explore Air 2 has a suggested retail price of $279.99 and is currently available online (as of 01/16/2018) at Amazon or other online retailers for prices ranging from $200-$250 (depending on availability and shipping costs). The Cricut Maker is currently available at Amazon for $179.99 with free shipping available when purchased directly from Amazon or any other online retailer such as Jet, Overstock, eBay, etc...

The cost savings on purchasing one or both machines will depend greatly on how often you will use them. If you are a person that will be creating more than just greeting cards with your pieces, then the Cricut Maker might be for you. If you only need to create cards and tags from time to time, the Explore Air 2 might be more appropriate. However, if you are someone who is constantly making scrapbooks for family and friends, the Explore Air 2 or even both machines may be appropriate depending on the cost savings of purchasing both machines in comparison to having one machine only.

The Cricut Maker may be typically used in conjunction with an iPhone or iPad, while apps can be downloaded from either Apple's App Store or most other app stores such as Google Play. Using the maker with an app allows for essentially limitless possibilities to create items ranging from greeting cards, invitations, postcards, gifts and any other type of material that would normally require multiple printed copies.

The Cricut Explore Air 2 is designed to work with the iPhone, iPad, Android smartphone or tablet. In order to use an app, you will need a Bluetooth compatible phone or tablet in conjunction with your machine. For best results, the Explore Air 2 should be used within 30 feet of your phone/tablet.

Included: The Cricut Maker comes with a starter pack of 6 assorted colors and 12 sheet protectors that come in handy for adding embellishments such as rhinestones, stamps, or badges to your work. This starter pack also includes a plastic cartridge that contains the Cricut Maker itself and serves as the main power supply for both machines when combined together.

The Explore Air 2 includes stamp pads, which can be purchased separately from various retailers for anywhere from $10 to $15 per set, depending on what design you want to create as well as where you purchase them from.

Storage: The Cricut Maker can be stored under a bed, on a table, or in another area where space is limited.

The Cricut Explore Air 2 will require approximately 24" wide of open space in order to allow for the side loading of cards and materials. The machine includes an opening on the side where you will insert your material slowly so that it is properly aligned for cutting. The machine also has a small, lightweight stand that can be stored underneath the cutting arm on the machine itself, which allows it to stand upright when not in use.

Line of Sight: While the Cricut Maker does not require you to have a line of sight for operation, you cannot use the Bluetooth feature to create designs unless you are within 30 feet of your device. The Explore Air 2 allows for wireless cutting with a compatible device anywhere that your phone or tablet can connect to the internet.

What is included: When purchasing either machine, only one cutting arm is included, and there are no other accessories or replacement parts that come standard with this initial purchase.

The Explore Air 2 will also include a wireless power adapter if purchased through Amazon. Verify with various retailers whether they will include a USB cord as well as which type is required for compatibility before making your purchase if it is not included with the machine.

Accessories: Both the Cricut Maker and Explore Air 2 accept many different types of materials for cutting and embossing. The machines are compatible with cutting mats, thin metal sheets as well as a variety of papers, including cardstock, vellum, and more. Each machine will come with several sample mats that include scalloped shapes such as hearts or flowers to test each side of the blade.

After this initial testing period, you can begin to experiment with different materials until you find your favorite combination of projects that will look great on your product as well as save you time during the process.

If you opt to purchase an additional blade for either machine, the Explore Air 2 has 5 blades available, while the Cricut Maker only comes with one standard blade for all projects. Additional blades can be purchased at various big box stores such as Target or Walmart in addition to online retailers such as Amazon or eBay.

If you need to replace the cutting blade for either machine, you will most likely need to purchase the entire top cover of each machine separately in order to access the blade itself. This is because there are no replacement parts that are available at this time for these machines unless you opt to purchase a second one as well. While it is possible to take a knife and cut out the side of the machine, it is recommended that you try to avoid doing this unless absolutely necessary, as it can be difficult and dangerous if done incorrectly.

Environmental Impact: Both machines produce less waste than traditional paper cutters. The Cricut Maker leaves no waste behind while creating blank cards or tags, but still has a limited amount of waste created while cutting certain materials aside from making basic shapes such as hearts or flowers with its blades.

The only other materials that must be purchased separately are any additional blades you may need in addition to the main cutting blade itself or any stamp pads you may want to use, depending on your projects and preferred layout.

The Cricut Explore Air 2 uses a similar concept as the Cricut Maker, except there is less waste created as you can reuse your cards and materials for various projects. The only additional supplies you may need to purchase are replacement stamp pads in order to create multiple stamps with the same stencil sheet or color ink cartridges in order to change the colors of your stamped work.

Footprint: If you are placing your machine on a tabletop or under a bed, the Cricut Maker would be the most practical option. This machine is lightweight at approximately 9 pounds and measures 16" x 10" x 4".

The Cricut Explore Air 2 does not require floor space for use but does require 24" of open space for side loading materials after cutting. The machine itself measures 12 ½" wide by 14 ½" deep by 11" high, so it is about 3 inches taller than the Cricut Maker; however, this extra height allows it to cut and emboss while standing upright on its own sidewise stand that can be hidden away when not in use, so you have less clutter around your workspace. The machine itself weighs 5 pounds, so it is lighter than the maker but still a bit heavier than the Explore Air 2.

Many people will spend hundreds of dollars outfitting a room with large areas and furniture to surround one of these machines in order to prevent any unnecessary friction and scrapes from arising from where you are cutting materials.

However, this can be extremely time consuming and could cost a lot more money if you want to buy high-quality products quickly enough. The Cricut Maker is compatible with most tablets, smartphones or iPads that are Bluetooth compatible such as an iPhone or iPad. You can download apps for both your apps store as well as other online retailers such as Google Play (for Android devices) or iTunes (for iPhone and iPad users).

While the Explore Air 2 is designed to work with iPhone or iPads, there are many free apps that allow you to create and design on your iPads mini or larger screen.

CHAPTER 6: CHOOSE THE BEST ACCESSORIES FOR CRICUT MAKER

When you have your Cricut, anything there is to know can be quickly overwhelmed. There are so many tools and resources to work with! How do you know what you're going to buy? How do you know what tools and crafts are most helpful to you? We were there, and we would like to help you out! In this post today, we'll show you 10 Cricut devices we use in our crafts faithfully.

Weeder

This tool is a must have for Cricut craftsmanship!

If you don't know about weeding yet, you're going to be early. Essentially, you need to remove unnecessary materials from your template and from inside when your Cricut cuts materials such as vinyl or iron-on. You eliminate negative space to achieve your design. In your life, you will need a weeder, trust me.

Basic Tool Set

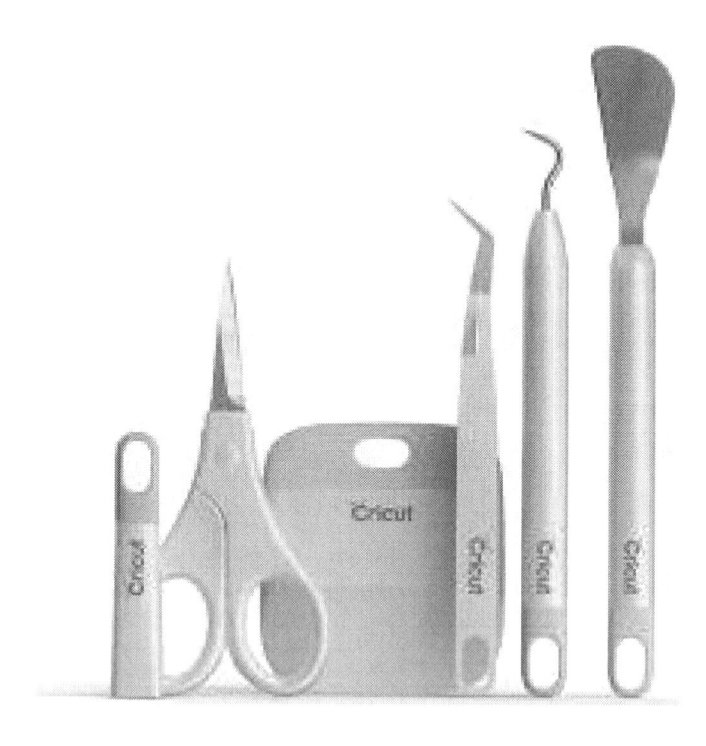

One of our most popular tool kits is this five-piece tool kit. This is a great tool to get when you start in the Cricut world!

We already spoke about how fantastic the scraper and the weeder are, so now let's look at the other three instruments. First up, scissors. I think how you will use this in your Cricut crafting is pretty obvious! The tweezers can then be useful to apply small information on your projects, weaken vinyl/ iron-on or remove hot carrier sheets. And finally, this pack also contains a spatula. This is another basic tool—it will help you to remove your mat materials! All in all, I would suggest to beginners the Simple Tools Kit. It'll help to get your Cricut craft going!

Brayer

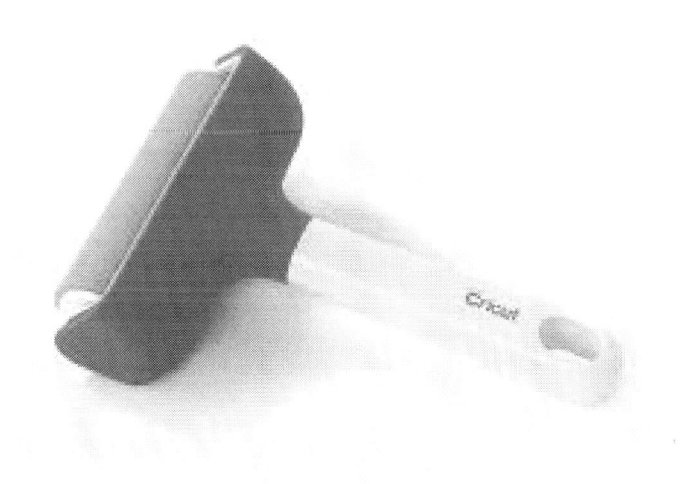

The brayer tool has been one of my favorite tools lately! The brayer was originally designed to help the Cricut Makers cut fabric, but there are many uses, even if you haven't got the maker.

I love to use the brayer to help the mat add materials. You may say, "Did you not just tell me to place materials on the mat using a scraper?" And yes—I did, but I think that the brayer is better for certain materials than the scraper. For example, I always apply leather and fabrics to my mat with the brayer tool. I don't know how to describe it, but the materials are safer for the mat when I use a brayer for materials like this instead of a scraper. I assume it has to do with the friction and how the materials are flowing. I use the brayer when I use a material I don't want to scratch.

For example, I recently did a project with adhesive foil. As I applied it to the mat for the first time, I used a scraper and figured out that I was scratching the foil. For the second time, I had to recut the material and used a brayer to scratch it. The scratching has only ever been done with foil, but I believe it is necessary to be extremely careful. All this to say, I love having the brayer on hand!

Scoring Stylus

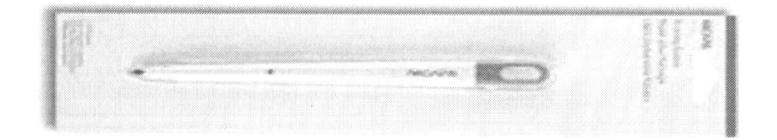

The scoring stylus is an excellent tool if you want to do paper projects! The scoring style is maintained by your Cricut to create fold lines for you. You now render tickets, envelopes, 3D boxes, and more easily! Both the Cricut Explore Air 2 and the Cricut Maker work for the scoring style. On a side note, you can use the scoring wheel for my Maker mates. Any of them works well.

Portable Trimmer

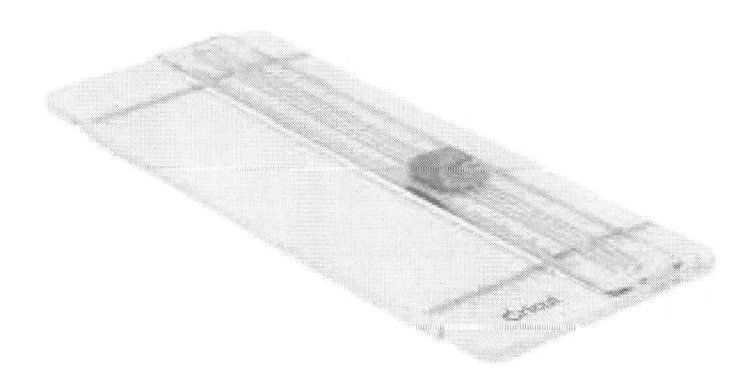

This trimmer is a GAME, you guys, CHANGER. You always have to cut pieces off when you work with materials, right? Can you even make straight lines! Honestly, though, I like using it as it helps me to hack and hack exactly what I need. And you can easily calculate what you need to cut on the trimmer so that exact cuts can be made! A swing-out arm helps you be straight, weigh, and cut your materials to exactly what you need. I think it saves a lot because you're cutting just what you need.

It comes with the trimmer and all the tools we spoke of earlier (scissors, scraper, spatula, tweezer, and weeder) in the standard toolkit, and it also has a score design. It's your buck's best bang, and you get a lot of devices. I had purchased this kit at the same time when I bought my Cricut and still using all the devices to this day.

Sewing Kit

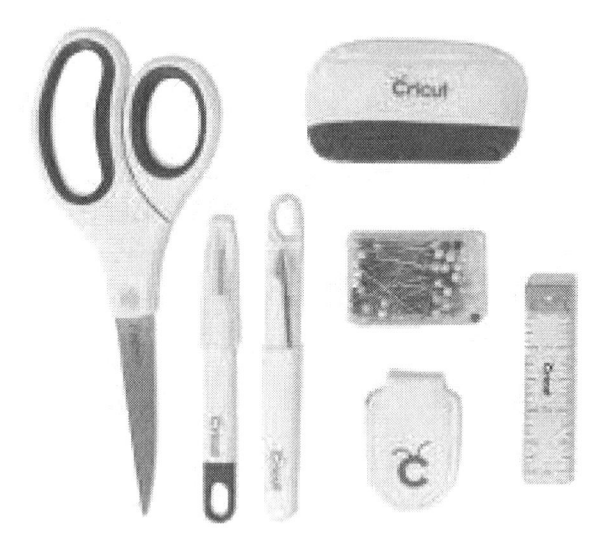

Cricut Creator can cut the cloth. It's very unbelievable technology! I also picked one of the sewing kits when I first got my Maker. If you're an avid sewer already, you may have many of these items. But I highly recommend this kit if you are new like I was or need to store some sewing pieces. There are seven pieces: a pincushion, shears for cloth, seam rivets, snips, pins, tape measurements, and a thimble of leather. All the pieces for your Cricut sewing + crafts!

Self-Healing Rotary Mat

They are 18" x 24" in two colors: mint and rose. One side has stunning architecture, and the other has a 30, 45, and 60-degree grid. I purchased the mint because it exactly suits my mint Air 2! All of this to say, I want to use this mat to carve up and cut the fabric. You're sure you're going to love it!

True Control Knife

The True Control Knife is last but not least. This is a Xacto, but WAY better! When using the True Control Knife over a Xacto knife, you can control your ventures better. You can cut a wide range of materials such as paper, cardstock, fine plastics, linen, fabric, and more. It has a rubber handle that helps you take a good hold, and it is equipped with five replacement blades that you can change quickly without touching the blade. It's a small but powerful device. Ten Cricut tools are great additions to your business room. My biggest piece of advice in determining which instruments to buy, you have to ask yourself, "how do I use this in my craftsmanship?" or "what do I want to do with this tool?"

Best Cricut Ideas into Your Cricut Projects

Are you looking for some Cricut projects? Here are some Cricut ideas for you.

How do you not start making wonderful projects such as personalized greeting cards now that you own your Cricut cutter? Start selling at local craft shows, online, or in specialty shops in your area.

Everybody could use a little extra cash today. Your first of several Cricut projects will have a set of approximately 10 to 12 cards. Be innovative; you can think of a lot of ideas. You must have a couple of birthday cards in this range (make sure you make cards for women, men, and children); make sure that Thank You, New Year's Day, Get Well, and even a Sympathy Card is included.

For some more projects, you can have your Cricut cutting machine to make blank note cards at any time. You may have card ideas like flowers on the cover with a rhinestone base or even the word hello with some other shapes. You can pack them in 4–6 card sets. All styles of tasks are at the touch of a button with your Cricut cutting unit. All kinds of ideas pour from the imaginative mind. You can even create decorated boxes in which to position your cards.

You now have to take your project Cricut together with some of your ideas, take them to some shops (florists, bakery, lounges, and small gift shops), and talk with the owner. Have your prices for every owner of the shop open. Make sure the price sheet is customized with the name of the company you are selling.

You will find yourself looking like a very professional businessman and not only an artisan trying to sell ideas for your card. Some owners can even leave your cards in their shop and take a percentage when they are sold. (What a better place for you to display your Cricut cards than 95% of the women who are, by the way, the best shoppers. Besides, those cards I sold in those shops. I have also received special baby showers and birth advertisements.) Don't forget to leave your business in the past! For special orders, customers may want to contact you personally. You can also sell online at a great place called Shop Handmade because it's free. Or at local art shows, you can even sell your Cricut designs. Don't forget Christmas and other great holidays that people send cards like Valentine's Day, Easter, Mother's Day, or Father's Day, while creating your cards.

You can also make a personalized baby shower, wedding shower, or even a wedding invitation for a few other projects with your Cricut cutting machine. There are so many ideas for cards of this kind. There are many Cricut cartridges specially designed for these projects. The Cricut Solution series contains a cartridge called Wedding for all the wedding shapes you can think of and also a Home Accent cartridge with lovely swirl shapes and flowers that you can also use for wedding purposes. If you decide to go along the route of Baby Shower or Birth Announced, big cartridges like the New Arrival will be released soon.

Whichever route you take, render many samples in different types. Call the nearest wedding planners, bakeries, florists, and baby shops. Take them for the wedding shows. I can't stop thinking of ideas. For a fantastic project, I had just another one. See, I said that once you start using your Cricut cutting machine, your ideas will start to flow. If you have any children's birthday party centers in your area, you can offer decorated bags and custom name tags. Display samples of different subjects (depending on your Cricut cartridges.) You can also make a catalog to leave so that consumers can see the options you have to sell.

The same core machine with additional features, strength, and project options:

- Rotary Blade – to cut fabric and all kinds of delicate materials.
- More Storage – The original Explore storage is new and improved to give more options.
- Device holder and charger – space on top of the machine to hold your devices and a charging port so you can charge while you create.
- iOS AND Android apps – both iOS and Android users can create on the go!
- Beautiful Design Details – same beautiful design with added details and just a tad bigger than the original Explore.

CHAPTER 7: CRAFT IDEAS FOR YOUR CRICUT MACHINE

Custom Graphic T-shirts

First, you will need to determine what you want your shirt to say. It is best to stick with just one color when you start. But as you get better at creating with your Cricut, you can move on to more color options in one design. Next is to pick which shirt you would like to use. This can be a preexisting shirt from your closet, or it could be one that you purchased specifically for this project. The shirt needs to be a material that can be ironed.

Supplies Needed:
- The Cricut machine
- Vinyl for the letters
- Your Cricut tools kit

Instructions:

1. Start by choosing the image you want to use. It can be done in Photoshop, or you can place your text directly into the Design Space.

2. Next, open the Cricut Design Space. Choose the canvas you wish to use by clicking the Canvas icon on the dashboard, located on the left-hand side. Select the canvas that you will be using for your vinyl letters. It can be anything within the categories they offer.

3. Then, select the size of the shirt for the canvas. It is located on the right-hand side of the options.

4. Now, click Upload for uploading your image, which is located on the left-hand side. Select the image you are using by browsing the list of images in your file library. Then, select the type of image that you have picked. For most projects, especially iron-on ones, you will choose the Simple Cut option.

5. Click on the white space that you want to be removed by cutting out. Remember to cut the insides of every letter.

6. Next, be super diligent and press Cut Image instead of Print first. You do not want to print the image. You cut it as well.

7. Place the image on your chosen canvas and adjust the sizing of the image.

8. Place your iron-on image with the vinyl side facing down on the mat and then turn the dial to the setting for iron-on.

9. Next, you will want to click the Mirror Image setting for the image before hitting go.

10. Once you have cut the image, you should remove the excess vinyl from the edges around the lettering or image. Then use the tool for weeding out the inner pieces of the letters.

Now you will be placing the vinyl on the shirt.

1. And now, the fun part begins. You will get to iron the image onto the shirt. Using the cotton setting, you will need to use the hottest setting to get your iron. There should not be any steam.

2. You want to warm the shirt by placing the iron on the shirt portion to hold the image. This should be warmed up for 15 seconds.

3. Next, lay the vinyl out exactly where you want it to be placed. Place a pressing cloth over the top of the plastic. It will prevent the plastic on the shirt from melting.

4. Place your iron onto the pressing cloth for around 30 seconds. Flip the shirt and place the pressing cloth and iron on the backside of the vinyl.

5. Flip your shirt back over and begin to peel off the sticky part of the vinyl that you have been overlaying on the shirt. This will separate the vinyl from the plastic backing. It should be done while the plastic and vinyl are hot. If you are having trouble removing the vinyl from the plastic backing, then place the iron back on the part that is being difficult. Then proceed to pull up, and it should come off nicely.

6. This should remove the plastic from the vinyl that is now on the shirt. Place the pressing cloth on top of the vinyl once again and heat it to ensure that it is good and stuck.

Wall Decals

Supplies needed are as follows:

- Adhesive vinyl
- Cricut machine
- Weeding tool
- Scrapper tool

Instructions:

1. Log in to the Cricut design space.
2. Create a new project.
3. Click on Upload Image.
4. Drag the image to the design space.
5. Highlight the image and "flatten" it.
6. Click on the Make It button.
7. Place vinyl on the cutting mat.

8. Custom dial the machine to vinyl.//
9. Load the cutting mat into the machine.
10. Push the mat up against the rollers.
11. Cut the design out of the vinyl.
12. Weed out the excess vinyl with a weeding tool.
13. Apply a thin layer of transfer tape on the vinyl.
14. Peel off the backing.
15. Apply the transfer tape on the wall.
16. Smoothen with a scraper tool to let out the air bubble.
17. Carefully peel off the transfer tape from the wall.

Make Stickers with Your Cricut

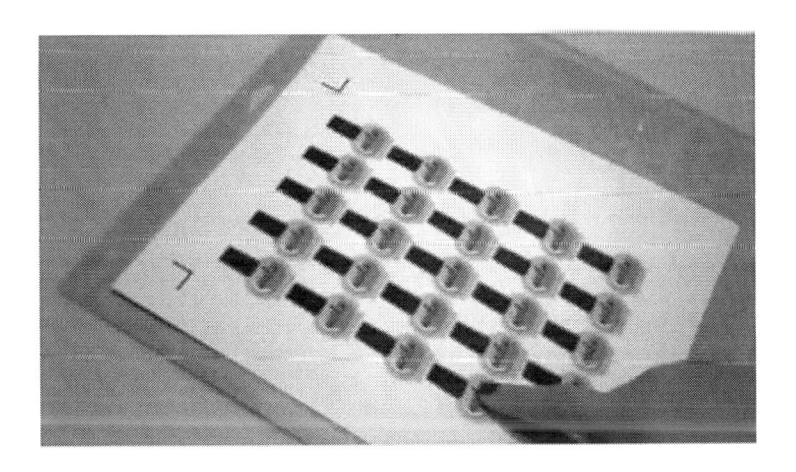

The supplies that you will need:
- Cricut Explore Air 2
- Printable sticker paper by Cricut

Instructions:

1. Log in to your Cricut Design Space account.

2. In the Cricut Design Space, you will need to click on Starting a New Project. Then, select the image that you would love to use for your stickers. You can use the search bar on the right-hand side at the top to locate the image that you want to use.

3. Next, click on the image and click Insert Image so that the image is selected.

4. Click on each of the files in the image file, then click the button that says Flatten at the lower right part of the screen. This will turn the individual pieces into one whole piece. It prevents the cut file from being individual pieces for the image.

5. Now, you want to resize the image so that it is the size that you wish it to be. This can be any size within the recommended space for the size of the canvas.

6. If you want duplicates of the image for sticker sheets, you should select all and then edit it and click Copy. This will allow you to copy the whole row that you have chosen. Once you have copied, you can then edit and paste the multiple images to make a sheet. It is the easiest way to copy and paste the image over and over again.

7. At this time, you are ready to start printing your stickers. Click the Save button on the screen's left-hand side to save the project and choose Save as Print and then Cut Image. Once done, you can click the green button that says Make It. This will be located on the part to the right of the screen.

8. Verify that everything is how it needs to be and click Continue. It will give you a prompt to print the image onto your paper. Make sure you have used the sticker paper for the stickers. Otherwise, it won't work.

9. Print out the image with your printer. If the Cricut sticker paper is too thick for your printer, using a thinner sticker paper is acceptable.

10. After the design is printed, adjust the Smart Set dial to the appropriate setting. Place the paper onto the cutting mat and load it into the Cricut machine by pushing against the rollers. Press your Load and Unload button that is flashing.

11. Press Go, and this will begin to cut your stickers. Since the stickers are small and intricate, you will need to be patient.

12. A tip for getting a good cut is not to touch the mat and once the first cut is made and done, repress the flashing button to re-cut the stickers on the same lines that were previously cut.

Making Planner Sticker

Supplies needed are as follows:

- Cricut machine
- Printable sticker paper
- Inkjet printer

Instructions:

1. Log in to the Cricut design spaces.
2. Start a new project and click on the Images on the screen's left side. Select the image(s) you want.
3. Click on the Text icon and input your text.
4. Select the font of your desire from the available font package.

5. Highlight the texts and change the color by using the available colors on the color tray.
6. Click on the Print option to change the file from a cut file to a print file.
7. Click on the Ungroup icon to adjust the spacing of the text.
8. After adjusting the spacing, highlight all and use the Group icon to make them one whole piece again.
9. Click on the Shape icon and insert a shape.
10. Change the shape's color using the color tray.
11. Highlight the text and use the Align drop-down box.
12. Make use of the Move to the Front icon to move the text to the front.
13. Highlight the design and click on Group.
14. Highlight the whole image and use the Flatten button to solidify the design as one whole piece.
15. Resize the design to the appropriate size you need. You realize this by clicking on the design, then dragging the right side of the box to the size you desire.
16. Click Save at the top left to save your project. Save it to be a Print and Cut image, after which you click the Make It button at the right hand of the screen.
17. Examine the result and click Continue if it's what you expected. It will lead you to print the design onto the paper.
18. Adjust the dial on the Cricut machine to the required settings.
19. Place the sticker paper on the cutting mat.
20. Load the cutting mat into the machine and push it against the rollers.
21. Press the Load/Unload button and then the Go button to cut the sticker.
22. Your planning sticker is ready.

CHAPTER 8: SOME WORKS YOU CAN DO WITH CRICUT MAKER

Cricut Maker Projects

The Cricut Maker machine is one of the most loved creating instruments. Which only a couple of steps, you can rapidly make a wide range of activities with various materials. Include additional accessories and devices, and your choices show signs of improvement. I cherish utilizing the pen to draw and compose with my Cricut. I also like utilizing the blade edge to cut thicker materials like basswood and turning edge to cut texture.

DIY Mini Felt Stocking Gift Card Holder

When you want to make endowments, however, don't have time, a DIY smaller than normal felt stocking gift voucher holder is impeccable. This smaller than usual felt stocking gift voucher holder rushes to make and easy to modify. It's a Cricut Christmas venture, so you realize it's fast to make. Give your Cricut a chance to do all the cutting with you, to do all the innovative things.

Make a small scale stocking gift voucher holder in not more than minutes.

Switch up the hues effectively with these smaller than expected tights. Pick your preferred felt and iron-on vinyl, and you're prepared to make adorable gift voucher holders. You can personalize the task include a name or a maxim utilizing iron-on vinyl. You can set up a wide range of embellishments and content cuts with your Cricut machine and Cricut Design Space. At that point, you should iron and present your adorable creation!

Materials
- Cricut machine and Cricut Design Space
- Stocking task canvas

- Red felt (utilize Cricut's making felt)
- Green foil iron-on vinyl
- Iron or EasyPress
- Cotton balls
- Glue
- Optional: Additional embellishments like sparkle or lace

Note about paste: Use heated glue to collect your stretchy and fluid art paste to follow the cotton balls. You can utilize whatever paste you like.

Directions

1. Go to the Stocking gift voucher holder venture canvas in Cricut Design Space. Adhere to onscreen guidelines to cut every one of the pieces and materials you need.

2. In case you're truly in a surge, design the front of the legging.

3. Glue the hanging circle to within, a backboard of the legging.

4. Assemble your legging, following the different sides together with paste or sewing. Ensure you leave space for the gift voucher to fit into the legging through the top.

5. Adhere the cotton balls to the highest point of the front of the legging to make the stocking "lighten." I discover it extends the cotton balls before sticking to make that cushy look.

Charming Donut Reading Set

You can make a bookmark and perusing log with your Cricut and a free SVG cut record set I've designed for you. This charming Cricut undertaking rushes to make. Print and cut each piece, or make your custom doughnut understanding accessories.

The doughnut SVG cut document set incorporates every one of the pieces you have to make a fun understanding unit. You'll prepare a to-print understanding log, two styles of bookmarks with cut accents, just as three doughnut designs you can alter to utilize any way you'd like.

Materials
- Cricut Machine and Cricut Design Space
- SVG and printable records
- Printer
- Twine (discretionary)

Instructions:
1. Ungroup the pieces. Resize and arrange any way you'd like. If you'd like the cut to emphasize on the doughnut bookmarks, layer the cut layout over the planning printed bookmark design. Utilizing the "shape" work, expel the external cut line of the cut format. Join the two layers together.
2. Follow on-screen directions to print and cut all your perusing set pieces.
3. Optionally, string twine through the top opening of the three doughnut bookmarks.

Entertaining Penguin Christmas card

Make a charming minimal amusing penguin Christmas card with my Rudolph penguin craftsmanship and send a little grin to companions or family. You can blend and match cardstock hues to make your very own look and browse ten changed penguins accessible in the Cricut Design Space library. Don't hesitate to switch up the shades you use for this Cricut venture or pick an alternate penguin to use with this card.

Materials
- Cricut Explore Cutting Machine
- Reindeer Penguin

- 12″ x 12″ StandardGrip Cricut® tangle
- Cardstock in occasion hues
- Silver and Red Cricut Pens
- Glue

Guidelines

1. Cut designs are adhering to on-screen guidelines.

2. Using glue, stack all the penguin patterns and top with the craft print. At that point, cut penguin design to make a dimensional complement for your card.

3. Glue a square pattern inside the front of the card, making a point to cover the square pattern window.

4. Optionally, cut out a second inside square to

5. Glue the penguin complement inside the window zone.

6. Assemble envelope.

7. Glue the smaller than expected heart to the focal point of the snowflake pattern design and use it as a sticker to seal the envelope.

Tip: Make more penguin cards! This reindeer penguin craft organizes with 9 other penguin designs accessible in the Cricut Design Space library.

Projects to Create Fabric Cuts Thanks To Cricut Maker

In case you're attempting to extend your innovativeness for utilizing the Cricut Maker, there are numerous tasks that you can take on with unlimited potential outcomes.

There are numerous extraordinary things about the Cricut creator machine that will make you need to utilize it to an ever-increasing extent.

Even though there's a wide assortment of undertakings, utilizing your creative mind for DIY activities will demonstrate that you have an imaginative and one of a kind eye with regards to using this machine.

We cherish utilizing the Maker for texture ventures.

One of the significant selling purposes of the Maker is that it can cut through the material because of its included Rotary Blade. Adopt the best hints on the best way to cut texture with the turning cutting edge here.

The rotational cutting edge is one of the 6 sides that work in the Cricut Maker. This cutting edge has a unique floating and moving activity (together with a large 4kg of power), which takes into account very sharp and clean-edged texture cuts. It accompanies a texture cutting mat, so you can cut a wide range of textures without utilizing any support.

Texture Projects to Try with your Cricut Maker

1. Blankets

The Cricut group has been making propels in bettering its design quality for blanket making. Cricut has cooperated with Riley Blake Designs to give crafters a wide assortment of sewing designs inside the example library. You can precisely remove the correct examples for sewing and make the ideal blanket easily.

2. Felt Dolls and Soft Toys

You might need to make toys without anyone else as a DIY. The Cricut producer effectively enables you to cut examples for delicate felt dolls and fragile toys. You can make a wide range of dolls for your children. Aren't these two above unbelievably sweet!?

3. Infant Clothes

The Cricut Maker can slice boards up to 12 X 24″. So while it will be dubious about making grown-ups garments with it, it is extraordinary for making infant dress. Make and slice designs, so you to make child shirts, onesies, shirts, and that's only the tip of the iceberg.

4. Doll Clothes

Since you're going to make dolls with the Cricut Maker, you can make them adorable little doll equips that will make them look increasingly one of a kind. Make a multicolor doll dress that will make your Cricut dolls stand apart among your locally acquired dolls.

5. Texture Christmas Projects (Ornaments and Christmas Stockings)

Utilizing the Cricut Maker will make cutting texture for making decorations and Christmas leggings a breeze. This machine is ideal for designing unique texture adornments or potentially leggings. The machine has an example library that you can use to mix various looks of Christmas or occasion improvements. Essentially utilize the machine to remove your example, and after that, sew it together.

6. Texture Appliques

Although you'll require a reinforced texture cutting edge in lodging, you can make a progression of texture appliques. These cutting edges must be bought independently at the same time when you have one. You can make a wide range of complicatedly designed appliques with your applique textures. Critical to note that, not at all like the revolving cutting edge, the reinforced texture edge requires you to have fortified support on your material.

7. Texture Key rings

Very easy to make and developing progressively well-known are texture key rings. There are easy designs in the example library. Dress your keys up with stylish texture key rings.

8. Texture Coasters

In case you're needing liners for your end tables or some other zone of your home, office or somewhere else, make them with the Cricut Maker.

9. Stick Cushions

It's conceivable you will do a ton of sewing with the Cricut Maker. As you get the majority of your lovely designs cut out, you're going to require a sticky pad to hold every one of your pins. There are diverse stick pad designs in the example library. As it is, you can get imaginative and make your own unique ones as well.

10. Pads and Cushions

Since the machine trims 12 X 24 estimated designs, you can make bunches of various pads and pads for your bed, chairs, lounge chairs, and niches. You can make a few incredible designs to tidy up your home. Remember that you can remove iron-on vinyl on your producer as well, so why not take your pad design to the following level.

11. Children Clothes

Why not prepare some uncommon things for your children. We cherish this DIY young men's bathing suit.

12. A Sewing Organizer for your Cricut Maker

Here is a sharp thought. Why not prepare a coordinator to keep the majority of your sewing supplies close by while you work with the Cricut Maker.

13. A Kids Backpack

Why not make an absolutely one of a kind rucksack for your girl or child? That way, you can topic it as indicated by their interests and interests, and you can add some flawless personalization to it too.

14. Producer Dust Cover

Another extremely astute thought. Why not make an unusual residue spread for your unique Cricut Maker machine. The machine is quite expensive, so you may very well also take care of it appropriately to guarantee that it works well for a while yet to come.

Select the spread design from your sewing library and sit back while the machine does its enchantment. While there are a lot of free examples in the Design Space library, you may prefer to consider getting a Cricut Designs Space membership.

CHAPTER 9: HOW YOU CAN MONETIZE FROM YOUR CREATIONS

How to Make Money with Cricut

There are countless things you can make with Cricut. Likewise, there are countless things you can make, which are marketable. Independent entrepreneurship is easier than it's ever been, thanks to the internet and web platforms that make selling your products a breeze.

You've likely already heard of some of the platforms that make it easy to start a shop of your own. Etsy is probably the most well-known of these platforms, and setting up a shop with them is so simple, it's almost impossible not to be interested in starting one for yourself!

With the Cricut, making countless items of every type and theme, for any and all occasions, is the name of the game. Doing these projects can be a huge source of joy for the avid crafter, but if you're spending the money on the materials for your projects, it might make sense for you to start generating a return on those, depending on how much you're doing and spending.

We'll cover some of the basics of what it means to go into business for yourself when you're the sole manufacturer of the goods in your store. Without having to provide a brick and mortar space for your shop, overhead can be so much lower than starting a shop or a store which is viable for people who might not have a lump sum of startup capital ready to hand.

How Do You Know When It's Time to Start a Shop?

If crafting is your passion, if you prefer to spend your time making items with your Cricut than you would going out or any other activity in your downtime, it could be time. If you're finding that your crafting room is getting full of projects you've made, but haven't gotten to use for that special occasion yet, you might find that you could sell those items to others, make back what you spent on the materials, as well as get paid for the time it took you to put the project together in the first place!

Should I Quit My Day Job and Go All In?

The thing about selling the products you create is that, since there's no brick and mortar location to manage, no store hours to keep to, you can manage your sales and your projects in the spare time that you have. It is best to start your store while you have a stable source of income. This way, as your store grows, you can scale back where it's necessary to do so in your usual work schedule to allow for more time to spend on your shop.

How Can I Make Sure People Will Buy My Products?

There is a wealth of ways to market a business in today's digital age. Between social media presence, search engine optimization and more, you can put your name everywhere it needs to be to generate interest. However, you might find that when you're starting out, it will be easiest to pick items that are not custom. Make a couple of each type of item, take stunning product photos, upload them to your store, and then sell those as off-the-rack items. As you start to generate more business, you may find that taking on the occasional custom order or commissioned item will benefit you. By and large, you will find that custom orders will take you more time and cost more to produce for less of a return. Be watchful of this, and if you find that making 100 of a general design and selling all of those is the best use of your time and resources, stick with that! There's absolutely nothing wrong with going that route.

Do I Need to Make Enough of Each Item in My Shop to Keep and Inventory?

The short answer to this is no. You don't have to make any more of any items that are being ordered at any given time. With the way Etsy works for sellers, you can determine how much time you have before shipping out an order, so you can make the items as they're ordered, so you can be certain you're never wasting product or letting it sit in your craft room for too long.

The only time it would be best to make any sort of inventory would be if you intend to rent a space or booth at a tradeshow or convention. Having a presence at craft fairs, conventions, tradeshows, etc., can generate impulse buys from passing patrons that could be great for your business.

If at all possible, it's best to wait to go to such an event until you're able to narrow down your best sellers. Once you have a smattering of items you can make that are your hottest items, you can make several of each of those and keep them at your booth or table, ready for immediate purchase!

Do I Need to Create a Shop in Order to Make Money with Cricut?

To be candid, no, you don't need to create a shop if you don't want to. There are always different ways of going about things and making money with your Cricut is as customizable as the Cricut projects themselves. If there is someone else who runs a craft shop, you might ask them to list your items for you in exchange for a share of the profits. You could create a partnership with a local school, community center, farmer's market or another establishment to sell your items for you to their patrons. There are so many ways to get your unique crafts into the hands of the public and to make money off the beautiful projects you make with your Cricut system.

Making an online store for your Cricut items might be the most direct, hands-on way to generate a stream of income from the items that you make. This does not mean, however, that it's the only way or that it's the best way for you to go about it. Test the waters, see what's available, and pick a path that is most workable for you and the business you're working to create.

How Should I Price My Items?

This, like everything else, is entirely up to you. One method of pricing is to decide on a rate you would like to be paid per hour spent on a project, multiply that rate by how many hours you spent on that project, and add it together with the costs of all the materials you used to do your project. For instance, I would never take a full-time job that paid me fewer than $15 per hour. We'll use this as our artisan rate to start. You can always adjust your prices as you get better with your craft, as you generate more of a following, and as you get faster at completing each of the projects you sell! So with this $15 hourly rate, we'll put together a little project. Let's say I'm taking a sheet of printable vinyl and printing an image that I own onto it. From there, I'm layering that vinyl onto a cardboard backing. Once that's done, I'm going to run it through my Cricut and make a jigsaw puzzle out of it. Once I've made my jigsaw puzzle, I'm going to use more cardboard to make a box, which I will then decoupage. The box will be filled with the puzzle pieces, wrapped with a satin ribbon, and sold in my online store. Let's run the tally!

Cricut Printable Vinyl - $9
Cardboard Sheets - $6
Decoupage Glue - $2
Satin Ribbon - $1
1 Hour of Labor - $15.00
Artisan jigsaw puzzle - $33.00

Do not sell yourself short on your labor costs, and do not charge less than you spend on your materials, ever! That's no way to run a business, and it's no way to live. Value your time properly and charge every penny that you're worth. With how beautiful your products are, you will find people will pay your rates, and you will get rave reviews every time!

What are the Best Platforms on Which to sell my Crafts?

This question is a little bit loaded and, what it boils down to is which platform is the most convenient, workable, and reliable for you. The business you want to create is going to take up a lot of your time and attention, so it's imperative that you're using a platform that fits all your needs, meets all your expectations, and solves more problems for you than it causes.

We can tend to be forgiving of quirks in new systems when we're learning them. However, take a little extra time to read the experiences and reviews of people who have used that platform for an extended period of time. This will give you a look into what your future could be like with that platform, and it's the only gauge you have to go by when it comes to how that platform will serve you.

You will want to spend a little extra time looking into which platforms are available, what costs are involved (if any), how they treat their sellers, what percentages of your sales are taken, and what the sellers on those platforms think of them.

Here are some of the top platforms you'll want to check into!

- Etsy
- Amazon Handmade
- Facebook Marketplace
- Folksy
  Artfire

- Craftsy
- eBay
- Craigslist

What Kinds of Things Can I Make with Cricut to Make Money?

You will mostly find that there are not any items you can make with your Cricut, which will not appeal to someone who would like to buy one. If you sell even one of each item you ever make, you're still coming out way ahead of the game, right? A lot of the items I'm about to list out for you are ones that can be purchased at a low rate from retailers, then customized using your design expertise, Cricut magic, and beautiful vinyl appliques that have sayings, monograms, or appealing designs on them. The choice is yours!

3D Puzzles

3D puzzles are made up of flat pieces that fit together to make a 3D object! Creating patterns for these that can be sold and assembled by your customers is a great way to capture the creatives in your target market!

3D Wall Art

Art that pops off the wall to greet you as you enter a room is a great way to create a dynamic décor that keeps people talking. Marketing art that jumps out at your target market is a great way to make an impression with people who are looking to you to provide a unique focal point for their interior design.

Aprons

Cooking enthusiasts love to have an apron that speaks to who they are as a chef or a baker. Blank canvas aprons are very affordable and, with iron-on vinyl that's available on the market today, from printable vinyl to glittery iron-on, there is no design you can't create to capture those creative cooks!

And so much more!

CHAPTER 10: CRICUT MACHINE MAINTENANCE & TROUBLESHOOTING

Blade Life

A blade can last between 500 and 1500 single cuts before it requires replacement. The life expectancy for a cutting blade mostly relies on the settings you use and the materials you cut. This is why you need to monitor the quality of your cuts, and when the quality decreases, that's when you will need to replace your cutting blade. In order to have the best possible results, make sure you only use Cricut Replacement Cutting Blades, available on the Cricut Shop, but also at other retailers.

Replacing the Cutting Blade

This is a process that you will definitely come across, especially if you are using the Cricut Machine on a frequent basis. Never replace the blade when the Cricut Machine is still on, in fact, you need to unplug it before replacing the cutting blade. After the machine is unplugged, you will need to take out the cutting blade assembly. Then, you will need to find the blade in the assembly and push it in, in order for the blade to emerge from the cutting blade assembly. Next, you will need to gently pull out the blade from the magnet that is holding it in place.

When you need to install a new blade, you will need to let go of the blade release and insert with caution the shaft of the blade in the hole at the bottom of the cutting blade assembly. Then, you will notice how the blade gets "sucked" inside the shaft and installed properly. Place back the cutting blade assembly into the Cricut Machine, following the reversed procedure of removing the cutting blade assembly. Please be aware that the cutting blades are very sharp and should only be handled with extra care. Also, they can be considered choking hazards, so you need to keep them away from children.

Replacing the Cutting Mat

Nothing lasts forever, and the Cricut Cutting Mat doesn't make any exception from this rule. It takes between 25 and 40 full cuts for a Cutting Mat to get damaged, and at that point, it should be replaced. The life expectancy of this spare part depends a lot on the materials you cut and the settings you use. When the paper is no longer sticking to the Cutting Mat, it has to be replaced. It's always better to replace the mat with genuine Cricut Mats, and it's perfect if you can purchase the Cricut Self Healing Mat. Always remember to rotate the mats to prolong the overall life of each mat.

Cleaning and Greasing Your Cricut Machine

Every product can show signs of usage, and a Cricut Machine may collect some paper particles and dust or you can even see grease from the machine building up in the carriage track. Luckily for you, cleaning up this machine is quite easy, but you need to consider the following tips first:

- Make sure you unplug the power from the machine first before cleaning it
- You can use a glass cleaner sprayed on a soft cloth to clean the machine
- If you notice static electricity build-up leading to the accumulation of paper particles and dust, all you have to do is to wipe it off with a clean soft cloth
- If you see grease building up on the bar across which the carriage travels, gently remove it using a soft cloth, tissue, or cotton swab

Machine Dial Not Working

If you ever come across issues with dialing on your Cricut Machine, you can just follow the troubleshooting steps below

When Explore Smart Set Dial doesn't turn:

- In this case, you will need to look for your proof of purchase (any receipt or invoice your might have regarding the purchase of this product) and prepare a short video of the issue
- You will need to Contact Member Care, using one of the options for assistance
- Unfortunately, there is no way to troubleshoot this issue

When the material is not changing in Design Space:

- Check the connection of the USB cable on both your Cricut machine and your computer
- Unplug the Cricut machine from the computer and then power it off. Next step, reboot or restart your computer. When the computer is back on, turn on the Cricut machine and reconnect it to the computer, then try to see if it's cutting again. If it still doesn't work, make sure you try the following step.
- Consider reconnecting your Cricut machine through a different USB port on your computer. If it still doesn't help, move on to the next step.
- Check if the issue happens with a different Internet browser. If the issue is happening regardless of the browser you are using, please consider the next step.
- Try to see if a different USB cable works (if you have a standard printer you can try it with that cable and vice versa), just to see if the Cricut machine can cut with a different cable. If your machine is in warranty and you don't have another cable, you might want to consider contacting Member Care.
- Check for any possible updates (make sure the Firmware is updated) on your Cricut Machine.

- If there are no available updates, please get in touch with Member Care for further assistance.

Machine Tearing or Dragging Materials

There might be situations when the machine has some malfunctions and it tears through the material. However, all these variables can be fixed using some basic troubleshooting steps. Therefore, if your Cricut machine is dragging or tearing through the material, make sure you check the following:

1. Check if you selected the right material setting in Design Space, or make sure that Smart

Set Dial is on the right setting:

a. if you are making a Custom setting, you can make sure that you select the right material from the drop-down menu

2. Check the intricacy and size of the image. When you are cutting an image that is small or very intricate, try cutting it larger or simpler.
a. If cutting a simple image fixes the issue, you can try cutting the more complicated one by using the Custom setting for Cardstock - Intricate Cuts.
b. If you are using Cricut Maker or Cricut Explore Air 2 in Fast Mode, make sure you disable the Fast Mode and reattempt the cut again.

3. Take off the blade housing from the machine, then the blade, and make sure there isn't any debris on the blade or inside the housing.

4. Decrease pressure settings for that specific material type in the Manage Custom Materials window by increments of 2-4. You can access the Manage Custom Materials screen from the account menu or by going to the Edit Custom Materials option from the upper right corner of the Mat Preview screen (just after clicking on Change Material).
5. It may have to be done 2-3 times in order to change the cut result.
6. Try to cut a different material (I would suggest copy paper) using the right setting for that material. Try to see if the problem is only with the material that you are trying to cut or the issue persists with other materials as well.
7. Consider using a new mat and blade. In this case, both of them can cause cut issues.
8. If you followed all the steps above, but the issues still persist, I encourage you to get in touch with Member Care for further assistance.

Machine Not Cutting Through Material

One of the most common issues of any Cricut machine is when it simply doesn't cut through the material, or it's just scoring the material, even though it normally should be cut without issues if it has the right settings applied. In this case, you only need to follow the troubleshooting steps below:

1. Check if the material setting you chose in Design Space or on Smart Set Dial matches the material on your machine mat. If you are using Cricut Explore models, you can go ahead with the Custom option and then select the right material from the Custom Materials list.
2. Go to the account menu and open the Manage Custom Materials page, and from this option, raise the pressure for your material setting by 2-4 increments. After this, try a test cut. You may have to increase the pressure settings by 2-4 increments 2-3 times to check if there are any changes in the cut result.
3. Try cutting a different material (the best choice would be printer paper), but using the right setting for the material. Do you still have the same issue? If not, then perhaps the issue lies within the original material you are trying to cut.

4. On your browser, you can also clear the cache and cookies and then try another test cut, and if the issue persists, may I suggest trying a different browser (I normally recommend Google Chrome or Mozilla Firefox).
5. If you have attempted all of the steps above and you still have issues, please get in touch with Member Care for further assistance.

CHAPTER 11: CRICUT TIPS, TRICKS, AND HACKS

Great job! You're almost through this book, and you're close to understanding everything you need to know about using Cricut cutters, creating amazing craftwork, and profiting with it. These final pages will let you in on useful little hacks that you can use with your Cricut to maximize material use, make creation easier, and save time. Here's what you can do to hack your way to seamless Cricut art…

Careful Peeling

When you're done cutting your materials, you are supposed to separate the material from the mat. Most people instinctively peel away the material from the mat. However, whether it's vinyl, cardstock, or adhesive paper, doing so comes at the risk of damaging or tearing your material. What you should do instead is curl the mat and peel it away from the material. Simply reverse the common step, and you'll preserve a lot more material than you otherwise would.

If you start creating products in bulk, you'll likely have quite a speedy production routine. Using this hack will ensure that you reduce material waste and have more quality products to market.

Careful Vinyl Storage

Storing rolls of vinyl can consume both space and time. If you don't have a good system, you could be spending hours each day rolling through different types of vinyl while you're trying to find the right one. Instead of having to look through dozens of different vinyl rolls each day, you can simply sort them in IKE bag storage holders. These convenient storage holders will allow you to sort your vinyl by color, type, or any other way you choose and make it easier to look through the rolls while you're working.

Keep Your Blade Sharp

Did you know that there is an easy way to sharpen your Cricut blade? All you need to do is use a piece of tin foil. Remove the blade from its clamp and run it through the tin foil between 10 and 12 times. This trick can significantly extend your blade's shelf life.

Organize Your Cricket Blades

In case you didn't notice, your Cricut has a place for you to store all of its add-on tools and small plates. You can safely store all the necessary tools and add-ons inside your machine when you're not using it. However, before you start using your Cricut again, make sure that there are no leftover tools that might intervene with the performance of the machine.

Easy Cleaning

Did you know that there is a simple and hassle-free way for you to clean glitter, paper, and vinyl scrap leftovers from your machine? It's true. All you need to do is run a lint roller through the side of your machine, and you will easily collect any small pieces of leftover materials. The same goes for your workspace.

Use Any Pen Brand You Want

If you don't want to use only Cricut's brand pens for your craftwork, the Explore Air 2 has an attachment that allows you to add any other pen to your machine. The best way to do this is to use a specially made pen adapter. With the Explore Air 2, you can find the adapters that will attach any other pan to your blade and ensure that it works well with the machine. This includes Sharpies, ink pens, and anything else you like. However, make sure to carefully read the instructions so that you attach the pen the right way.

The Vinyl Weeding Hack

Did you know that there is an easy and simple way to weed your vinyl scraps? All you need to do is get a nail polish holder and store the vinyl scraps there. No more mess at your workspace, and no more having to figure out different ways to store and collect scraps of material.

Find Software Freebies

Of course, Cricuts come with a free Design Space installation. So, why would you want any other software? As it turns out, there are a couple of them out there that require a subscription, but they do make the design process considerably easier. The best part is that you can find coupons and discounts for these all over the internet. Make sure to check out other apps as well to see if they have particular functions that would make your work easier. For example, some of them convert files effortlessly, while others let you design with more ease and convenience.

Store Supplies on a Pegboard

There are only a few types of boards that are as convenient as pegboards. These boards allow you to add hooks to them, then attach containers for any tools and supplies you need. This is a great way to organize, considering that these boards come at a fraction of the price you'd usually pay for an organizer. They have a couple of other advantages as well, though. They use up vertical wall space, meaning that no working space will be taken away from your office or workshop. Plus, they are highly adjustable, and you can move your containers around, add more, and remove them exactly as you need.

Easy Mat Cleaning

Cricut mats are simple to use, but they can pick up debris over time. Instead of throwing out your mat, you can effortlessly wipe it down with baby wipes and then spray a couple of layers of adhesive spray on it. You can easily get up to ten uses out of your mat if you use this method.

Vinyl Hack #2: Slap Bracelets

Working with vinyl is amazing, but organizing it requires a bit more cunning. There's another cheap way to keep your vinyl rolls together. All you need to do is fix them with slap bracelets, and you're done.

Wood Bin Material Organization

Rolls and rolls of paper, adhesive, glitter foil and other items can be a pain to organize. The fact that they can look very similar, and so it's possible to mix them up, is one more reason to give your organizing habits more attention. So, what's another way to organize your rolls of paper, vinyl, and fabrics? The answer is wood bins! The process is easy. You need a number of bins to match the type of materials. Just label the bins, and your work is complete.

Cut Materials with Straight Edges

If you're using an off-brand material with your Cricut, you're going to have to adjust the dimensions of the machine. As a result of this, you might end up with plenty of material waste. One of the ways to prevent this is to trim the sheets before loading them into the machine by using a straight edge. Neat, right?

Use Free Digital Resources

Did you know that there are multiple websites out there that offer completely free images and vectors? Why shop for designs when you can download them for free? The same goes for patterns and quotes.

Fix Materials with Painter's Tape

Having your thick materials slide on the mat can be frustrating. Luckily, there's a simple way to deal with this problem, and it is to use painter's tape. This tape will damage neither the mat nor your material, as it's made to be used on walls without ripping off their paint.

After you're done working on your project, you can just remove the tape, no flaws left behind. This hack is particularly great for wood and chipboard.

Use Transfer Tape for Neat Curved Surfaces

If you're looking for a way to keep your material smooth when making a curved surface, there's a very simple hack that you can use. What you need to do is cut slits around the edges of the transfer tape so that you can place the design with more accuracy. That way, there won't be any last-minute mess-ups just when you think you got your design right.

Write Down Your Cheats

Different materials on the Cricut require a different setting, adjustments, and add-ons when cutting, scoring, printing, and writing. If you want to work with a multitude of materials, and you don't want to get lost in the settings, print out your cheat sheet for the right add-ons and customizations for certain materials.

Chances are high that you won't be able to memorize all the functions, settings, and pathways for each of your projects. So, why not write or print out your cheat sheets? Having a reminder by your side will ensure that you won't get lost while you're trying to work on a project, and also that you won't set the wrong settings by accident. You can print your cheat sheet and keep it next to your laptop.

When planning a project as a beginner, it can also be useful to plan and write out your ideas for how creating the project is going to go, as well as the exact pathways in Design Space you'll use for the necessary settings. You can also write out which knives, pens, mats, and Design Space pathways to use when working on balsa wood, vinyl, paper, etc.

Use Magazine Holders

If you need to work on the go, and you require a limited number of materials for your project, it could be a good idea to store them in a magazine holder. This is an easy way to sort and carry your materials. You can stack or roll the materials as needed, and you can also further adjust the organizer by adding dividers and labels. Magazine holders are yet another solution for material organizing without having to spend money on brand-new organizers.

Use Adhesives on Wood

There's nothing better than combining beauty with quality in your craftwork. Adhesive vinyl can give just the right tone and texture to your creation, and you can also use it for adhering images, patterns, and quotes to almost any wooden piece. Arguably, balsa wood is one of the sturdiest materials to work on with Cricut, so combining the two will result in the best combination of quality, sturdiness, and beauty. You can use this combo on a multitude of projects and decorations, from pictures to lamps and even jewelry organizers. Don't forget to carefully choose the type of vinyl to combine with wood so that you don't end up with a cheap look.

Check Design Space for Freebies First

Do you need a new pattern or font? Make sure to check Design Space before purchasing anything to see if they have some freebies or discounts worthy of your attention. It may appear at times that those graphics you need to purchase are better quality compared to those that come for free, and you might be able to notice subtle differences from your end. But will other people be able to tell the difference, and will pay for a digital asset make any true difference to the quality of your products? Sometimes they will, but most of the time, there are perfectly fine freebies that you can download instead of paying. So why pay when you don't have to?

CONCLUSION

Thank you for making it to the end. A lot of crafters are using the Cricut Maker to create their own projects or home deco items like blankets & pillows, quilts & runners, etc. They also sell pre-designed projects on the website and in stores. Cricut has also released various product extensions, including free downloadable patterns & stencils for Cricut Maker and Silhouette, and a series of accessory sets: a needle book, zig-zag guide, ruler & color palette.

Cricut (cricut.com) is a company that focuses on crafting tools and machines. They began by supplying scrapbooking supplies, but now offer all kinds of products. Some of these include paper cutters, cutting mats, cutting systems and vinyl cutters.

It's a good idea to read the reviews and other information online before you purchase the Cricut Maker. It can be a bit daunting because it's so new, but it is simple to figure out once you get familiar with how it works.

As we end this book, here are some tips:

1. Read the instruction manual: Google has an awesome search function that can help you find information on anything from recipes to craft projects. You can use this as a guide after you figure out how to use the Cricut Maker at home for projects. There are many videos on YouTube showing how to use your Maker as well!

2. Take advantage of online resources: Check out websites like Pinterest (Cricut Design Space) and YouTube (Cricut tutorials) for inspiration! You can also check the Amazon website for information about products related to your Cricut Maker that may be useful for projects - there are lots of things available there! It's a good idea to keep this page open when using your machine and refer back again later if something doesn't go right or you're not quite sure how something works yet (or maybe even need some ideas!).

3. Be patient: After you've read the instructions, practice using the Maker on scrap fabric, paper or card stock until you are comfortable and know what all of the buttons do. Then it's time to create your first project! There's a tutorial video and a lot of online resources available to help you out with this. You will not be able to master it in one day, but it won't take very long before you feel more confident and begin experimenting on your own! Most machine users loved finding out how they could use their machine after they were familiar with it - the best advice is to stick with it!

4. Use something that can be cut easily: For example, if you want to make a patchwork quilt or pillowcase, then try out a piece of cotton fabric that has small patterns running through the piece already (such as batiks). This might make your job faster for cutting pieces for projects like these than trying to cut normal cotton or flannel.

5. Use a good machine: The Cricut Maker is really easy to use, but it is not the most durable machine you will find on the market. If you want to do more projects with this machine, then be sure to take good care of it. The cutter head is made of plastic and can wear out if you push down too hard or put too much pressure on it when cutting fabric or paper.

6. Read online reviews: There are many mixed reviews on Amazon about numerous products. Reviews from other online sources can help you figure out what this product is really like, what features are important to look for, and how it compares to the COMPETITION (Cricut Maker vs. Silhouette Cameo).

7. Check for coupons and sales: You can find great deals on the Cricut Maker by looking online at places like eBay or the Amazon marketplace. Many sellers will sell used or refurbished units, and they are usually a good deal! However, be sure to do a little research before buying from a website you're not familiar with - this is a great time to use that Google search function again!

8. Don't buy add-ons right away: The Cricut Maker isn't exactly cheap, so you don't want to waste your money on things that aren't crucial for using it. However, there are some really great accessories available such as extra blades, pre-made stencils & patterns for cutting fabric AND vinyl letters/numbers/designs, etc., specialty dies/punches you can use with your machine (such as alphabet dies), etc... The price of any add-on varies depending on the product. Sometimes you can get a great deal on these products (like 50% off!) by checking out other websites or buying them from individual sellers.

9. Try different colors: Some people prefer cutting out fabrics in one color to create one piece, but they want the opposite for their backgrounds. In this case, use two different colors, and you'll have more options!

10. Practice, practice, practice: Sewing and crafting is something that takes time to learn. You'll get better at using your maker with every project! Remember this is a fun hobby/pastime you are doing for yourself, so don't stress if it's not perfect the first time - experience is what counts!

11. Use safety and common sense when using your machine: Be sure to read the manual carefully before using it again and always be aware of where it is while you use it (the cord may be very long, so make sure not to accidentally cut or pull out too far and someone gets hurt).

12. Have fun! Get creative! Be sure to share your projects with us by posting pictures on our Facebook page or tagging us on Instagram.

13. Don't forget about the original Cricut Maker: If you're still in love with your first machine (that's really not a bad idea - they work perfectly fine still!), then you can still use all of the accessories and designs you already have for it with your brand new Maker! There is no need to get rid of it - you can use one for different things or keep both machines! The blades for the original will fit in the new Maker, so you will be able to cut fabric and vinyl, etc... You'll just have to make sure that any new material fits inside like ordinary paper.

I hope you have learned something!

CRICUT PROJECT IDEAS

A comprehensive guide to create amazing and easy projects.
Maser your cricut maker or explore air 2 with creative ideas

PAMELA CRAFT

INTRODUCTION

The Cricut machine is a craft cutting machine manufactured by Provo Craft. It is heavily marketed towards crafters and has been since its release in 2003. The Cricut offers users the ability to cut various adhesive-backed materials and custom-make signage, cards, gift tags and other crafting projects. However, it has developed a more niche following for users who enjoy making their own vinyl sticker skins for their Apple iPhone or iPad. These skins can be applied with heat from an ordinary hairdryer and will not damage the device surface underneath unless removed incorrectly (using alcohol or any sorts of solvents).

The term "Cricut" has started to be used to refer to the machines themselves, as well as the cut-paper sheets that are available for use with the machines. The words were coined by enthusiast Nicole Larkin, who was not affiliated with Provo Craft in any way. She started using the terms "Cricut" and "Cricut machine" in her YouTube video series on December 6, 2008 (LINK 1) and produced a song about them at Christmas 2008 (LINK2).

The Cricut was released as a consumer product on April 1, 2003, for about $299 USD. It was manufactured by Provo Craft of Salt Lake City, Utah. The first official public demonstration of the new machine came on May 3, 2003, at the Web 2 conference in New York City. At that time it cost about $450 USD.

A version of the machine called "The Cricut Maker" was released in 2004 and retailed for approximately $399 USD at some point after 2006 and before 2007 (there is no confirmation yet if this is still available). The Maker cuts paper instead of fabric or vinyl, such as stickers or decals. Maker uses an electronic motor for its cutting mechanism. The craft cutter cuts fabric and vinyl only, although this can be changed by purchasing a Cricut Blade for the Maker.

Manufacturer Provo Craft has sold over 100,000 units of the Cricut machine. The machine is often described as "limited edition", although Provo Craft has disputed this claim. As of 6 January 2006 (when they were expecting to sell about 1,500 units a month), Provo Craft had sold about 57,000 units worldwide and expected them to sell about 10,500 units per month in 2007.

The machines are manufactured in Utah with components from Taiwan and China. It's being manufactured with a special "inert" cardboard that means it cannot be recycled with normal paper products because of the toner particles used during manufacture; therefore, they are being manually archived by the manufacturer's facilities in Utah for proper disposal when the tool becomes obsolete or becomes damaged beyond repair (when they expect to begin selling replacement parts instead).

Beyond the initial release of the machine and its accessory items such as blades and paper trims, Provo Craft released a number of other products for the Cricut. These include:

All of these tools come with a refundable 25% restocking fee if you return any tool during one year from purchasing it (for example: if you purchased an XL Master Cricut tool on November 30th, 2005 and returned it on December 26th, 2005, after spending two months using it you would still be responsible for shipping and handling on November 30th). The 25% restocking fee is also waived if you cancel your order within 24 hours (during which time you can work out a solution with them to have someone else take over your order). Though orders placed after November 20th don't get this 25% cancellation fee because they count as "delayed".

Users of the Cricut enjoy using the machine because of its different and exclusive designs. Users can create a variety of projects with the use of their Cricut. Some examples include windows, journals or planners, invitations, or scrapbooks.

Cricut users have posted online tutorials on how to make many types of projects with their Cricuts online. Many websites were created to help people make their own designs.

While the Cricut is not a new tool, it has gained popularity quickly among crafters. Many people have their own "personal" Cricuts, which they create using the Cricut Design Space. It is important to note that these machines will be obsolete in 5 years or less. The Cricut Company plans to release a newer version of their cutting machine in 2009.

The machine is able to cut vinyl and fabric, as well as paper (including stickers and tags). The Cricut cutting machine is an electronic machine that cuts patterns out of paper, fabric and vinyl. It can cut a variety of materials with adhesive backings. There are many kinds of blades for the machine that allow it to cut these different materials. Most recently they have introduced a blade for cutting wood and metal.

The Tool is composed of two parts: the main unit and the mat. The main unit consists of a power source, a tracking device, rollers, cutter blades and tracking wheels. The mat is similar to any other cutting mat in that it has an aluminum vinyl surface on which you can create your project if there's no surface underneath it (for example, on your desk). Using the Cricut Maker Tool to cut paper is very different from using the Cricut Machine. While the machine version has a top and bottom surface that interlock, the Maker Tool has an aluminum surface on which you can cut out patterns. You simply line up your design on top of your mat, then turn on the tool. The plastic trac-track wheels roll over the surface as you turn it on and cut out your project (if there's no material underneath it).

The Cricut Maker tool cuts through materials such as vinyl, fabric, paper and cold metal. The machine has a cutting edge that allows for very precise cuts (down to 1/32"/1 mm).

CHAPTER 1: WHY SHOULD YOU START USING A CRICUT MACHINE?

The Cricut machine can be used to make a variety of craft projects, including those for the home and office. It is a small cutting machine that is mainly used for paper crafting. The tool has been in existence since 2004. It was first produced by Provo Craft, Inc. in Provo, Utah. Since then, it has undergone some changes to its design but still maintains its functionality as a superior paper cutter.

Today's Cricut machine is much different from the older versions. The old version was designed to cut vinyl, not paper. When the machine came out in 2004, it was very unique because it cuts on a ruler system. This meant that there were no measurements or guidelines for the blades. It simply cut like a pizza cutter.

The original design of Cricut's machine was also very bare-bones, even though it had multiple options for dimensions and templates, such as cutting mat templates used in the school setting or paper cuts for decorating projects. Cricut offers new templates that can be used to cut things like gift tags and party favors, and vinyl, as well as other versatile materials. The newer model is called the Cricut Explore Air 2, which is a more developed version of the original model. The new model gives a user many more options on what they can make with their machine versus just cutting out shapes as they previously did before.

The Cricut machine is a cutter, which means that it cuts out shapes from paper. It cuts out vinyl and other materials as well. The machine comes with a variety of different templates that can be used to cut different materials, including, but not limited to, paper and vinyl.

There are many ways to work with the machine and the templates. The most basic way is to grab any of the template sets available for sale from Cricut's website or from Wal-Mart, Target, or other retail stores. There are a variety of packs available in every imaginable shape and size, from simple designs like Valentine's Day cards to more intricate designs for special occasions such as Christmas or New Year's Eve parties. There are also cookie-cutter templates available that can be used for baking purposes, such as cutting out cookies for homemade gifts or making holiday treats at home. There are even birthday party ideas available in different shapes and sizes that can be cut out by the user using this tool from Wal-Mart or Target.

The Cricut machine can be used to make a variety of different things in the home, including homemade gifts for friends and family. It can cut out tags that can be used for decorating homemade gifts or on items you may have purchased.

Home decor is one of the easiest ways to use the Cricut machine. There are many options available for creating home décor items, such as wall hangings, pillows, curtains, and many other choices. The templates available are very versatile and so easy to use that even young children can do it as long as they follow directions. Children love creating their own personal decorations for their rooms using this tool. It is a great hobby for them to have while they learn how to read and write as well as focus on some hand-eye coordination skills at the same time.

For office use, the Cricut tools make it easy to create signage or special promotional materials such as business cards that promote your company's name or specific products you sell in your office. The Cricut machine allows you to cut even the most intricate of designs with ease.

Another way to use the Cricut machine is for scrapbooking projects, especially in old pen and ink style. There are many options available on the market for scrapbooking, and many choices are made by either specific designers or at specialty stores.

The Cricut machine is one of many different ways that people can create homemade scrapbooks that they keep at home or that they give as a gift. Making note cards on the computer is a very popular option, and it can be easier to share with friends and family members who do not have access to a printer or computer and may not know how to make their own cards themselves.

There are a variety of other reasons why people use the Cricut machine besides cutting cards, crafts, gifts, etc. This tool has features such as a magnifying glass that allows users to see small details on templates prior to buying them so you can make sure you will like what you end up cutting out when using this product. Another feature of the machine is the ability to insert photos onto the cards. This makes it easy for people to personalize their cards by adding a photo from a family member or friend or even a cute picture of someone's pet that they want to remember.

The Cricut machine is an easy way for people to make their own unique scrapbooks for those who are interested in doing this type of project but may not have access to other types of software that can help them put pictures and text together. There are many different options available on the market from specialty stores and online retailers, such as Wal-Mart, Target, etc., and some templates are even specifically designed for scrapbooking in mind.

The Cricut machine has many features that make it fun to use in many different ways, depending on what you are cutting out for use on your project. One key feature is the ability to cut things like cardboard if you decide you want some extra support while working with your papercraft project. There are also several features that allow users to work with vinyl or other materials, which can be used with storing projects at home or giving them as gifts.

Cricut as a Hobby

A lot of women are now getting interested in scrapbooking and other arts and crafts. There are many women who enjoy the process of creating things with their hands. Many of them are now busy with making scrapbooks and also doing some handicrafts for their homes. Many women find Cricut fun because it is relatively easy to use, aside from being affordable. If you want to have a crafting experience, then you should never miss this modern machine that will surely make your work easier so that you can enjoy the whole process even more.

Cricut is just one of the many new toys that women can have when they are into crafting. It might be a little too modern for you, but if you are into technology, then this is definitely something you should get for yourself. This toy allows you to create different things in many shapes and sizes, and it's easier than ever before with Cricut. You can make your own stickers, cards, scrapbooks, invitations, and so much more that will make your friends unsure whether you are really making these or buying them from a store.

This machine can also be useful in cutting letters and making words on your own paper mache. You can trace the word on any type of paper or cardboard, such as plastic sheets that Cricut uses with its cartridges and then cut through the letters easily to make it stand out more than before. These letters will surely give any word some class that will set it apart from the others since there will be no scratches or lines visible on the letters' sides since the Cricut would have already made those tiny incisions for you already. This will make your scrapbook look more artistic, and it's an easy way to make things look better because of the amazing quality of the product.

Cricut is a great machine that you can use on different occasions for a variety of things, one thing that you must be careful when using is safety. Since this machine cuts through different materials, it is important to cut through them carefully since you do not want any accidents by applying pressure to the wrong part. Always try and cut with care, especially when using this as a gift for someone.

Do not cut anything or anyone without permission since many people have asked for injury lawsuits if something goes wrong with the product, even though an accident was already unavoidable. You can also refill cartridges by buying new ones from Cricut so you can make your own creations too if you are into this hobby. Cricut gives you many forms of designs and patterns that will fit perfectly on your papercrafts and card making projects, so just choose what kind of design will suit your needs the best at any time during crafting time or whenever you would like to create something unique for yourself.

A new and revolutionary craft tool, the Cricut, is revolutionizing the crafting industry. The Cricut has created a whole new crafter who is self-directed, motivated, and capable of creating an array of products from a single tool. The time spent creating products in creative ways is made possible thanks to Cricut's easy-to-use interface. The texture features also increase the fun possibilities with great results. The ease of use makes it an ideal craft tool for novice users as well as professionals.

Cricut's user-friendly features make it easy to create and produce goods. The Cricut produces products that are not only esthetically appealing but also functional as well. With the Cricut, crafters can churn out all sorts of products such as stickers, cards, scrapbooks, invitations, and so much more that are made from different materials. The Cricut's cartridges are used to make these products possible. These cartridges come in different shapes and sizes to help the crafter get inspired by a multitude of possibilities for personal use or commercial usage. There are also specialty cartridges that allow crafters to engrave specific words or images into their products.

Cartridges can be refilled using genuine Cricut blades so that the craftsman can create more things without having to buy new cartridges after finishing a single project. Cricut also provides professional-grade blades specially designed to work with the Cricut. These blades are available in various shapes and sizes that can be used to create all different kinds of things.

The Cricut is made of high-quality ABS plastic. This plastic is resistant to heat, and it allows for easy cleaning without damaging the machine. The machine can be used by people with arthritis since it does not cause pain upon contact, as well as those with dexterity problems since there is no need for any assembly or assembly steps.

Cricut's digital technology makes it possible to cut perfectly every time. The machine's cutting accuracy ensures that only one product will be produced, even when cutting several objects at once due to the design of the circular cutting pad on which the material is exposed for cutting. This ensures that there will be no waste or miscutting when cutting various products at once, provided that they use a cartridge from the same company.

CHAPTER 2: MAKE MONEY WITH CRICUT MACHINE

Selling for Profit

The lower the craft, the more lucrative it is when selling art. It turns out. Fewer expenses for shipping, less material, everything works out. Therefore, my main concern is the cost of equipment, overall size and transport aspects, effort (as time is money!), and popularity.

Material cost - Material expenses are usually priced, but overhead expenses are something you might want to consider. Most individuals must pay the cash first to purchase products. Some unused scraps and materials will also be available when you buy bulk. You can always try and buy only as much stuff as you need, but it is never optimized correctly.

Shipping - Many reports publish that shipping is free, and individuals purchase only more. It is generally feasible for the seller by folding the transport expenses into the price of the item. It is okay if you have a high-cost product, but it doesn't make sense to the end customer if the article's original price is $5 and the shipping costs 50.

Effort - It is mostly a work of love for most artisans who sell their goods. But when you make crafts for orders, your life gets away from the fun. It just has to be remembered. Do you want to weed it for an hour and sell only for $5 if you sell a complex vinyl piece? Popularity - fads are coming and going, it never hurts driving one.

Let's begin with the list:

Vinyl Crafts are the Most Lucrative

Cricut vinyl projects, the ideal material for company vendors in Cricut. It's comparatively cheap, lightweight, and effortless to ship, and most importantly, you can do so much.

Wall Art

Here there are endless opportunities. Even with Fixer Upper presently not showing, the decoration of the farmhouse's wall remains powerful. Pinterest searches for farmhouse wall arts are over half a million per month. Don't miss actions. Don't miss them.

Custom Decals

Custom stickers are great, as they apply from parties to home décor for many end applications. It is a difference that large retailers cannot compete with when you offer a tailor-made service.

Children Related Wall Decals

The decorations of the children occur throughout the year. There's a constant need to decorate babies and children from kindergartens to birthdays to baby showers.

The Wedding Industry is Alive and Well

The wedding industry that's not unexpected. The back yard marriages are on the increase, according to Pinterest. It has increased by 441% in the search. All try to save their friendship a little. I began with the Cricut Air to make cash from a Cricut Air 2. After I got my Cricut Maker on the Cricut Explorer, I discovered that most of my stuff accomplishes. So many products sell with the Cricut Explorer. Paper flowers' popularity is at an ever-high level, just like farmhouse decor, with over half a million searches per month on Pinterest. They are fantastic for every opportunity, from Mother's Day to Baby Shower's weddings. They're on-demand, no wonder.

Cricut Cake Toppers

Customization is a crucial case, and the toppers of the cupcake can be the most straightforward and most economical. Parents always try to raise their games at birthday parties for children with various personalized decorations and favors.

Leather Earrings

If you only want to test the water, go to a shop and use a batch of free leather swatches to create an original quantity.

Keep business accounting up to date.

Make your company a city, state, or county official. While I can't tell you precisely how to do this, there's an excellent starting point here—different in every country.

Keep purchasing impulses at a minimum in your company.

Pay off the debts of your company and avoid liability. Debt is no good—see how you can keep your company out.

Set up a company savings account automatically draft your company bank account.

Post to social media regularly.

Create and begin using a profile on a new social media network.

Start with a calendar of content.

Network to encourage your goods jointly with other tiny company owners.

Begin marketing for a new population. If you are presently producing goods mainly for mothers, broaden your marketing to include other groups of individuals.

Get out of the market and launch your website.

Buy a loyalty program for your clients.

Enhance your branding. You may have your logo, brand colors, packaging, etc..

Register for a course related to business.

I often hear from owners of small businesses that "my product photos are bad." Make it a better objective!

Contact your customers more to find out what they want. Whether social media or surveys, the best product is that which meets your requirements.

Start something new.

Create pop-up stores all year round to increase your company knowledge. Think of how many people you might attend for the year when you set a target—a month? A quarter by one?

Here are a few ideas.

Time Management

Enhance your balance of working life by setting and adhering to regular office hours. Hire your company's assistance. Hire assistance. Take some of your burdens from social media support to creation and packaging.

Plan your holiday. While it may appear counterproductive, it takes time to escape reality and charge all business owners. If you haven't been on holiday for years—this year, plan on it. Even better? Use artisanal cash to finance it.

Productivity

Set several goods each week or month to be produced. These can be products that are digital or tangible. Switch your custom store to the vessel ready. What do I believe about custom goods? Clean the things you don't need from your craft and maintain them tidy this year. Although this may be a good idea, you can increase productivity through a clean, structured workspace.

There are two main components to set objectives:

1. The goals that you set must be realistic and achievable. If you're just beginning, sales of $100,000 in your first company month are not practical. But in the first month of the company, it is feasible to set a $1,000 sales target.
2. If you set them and forget them, the objectives are not right. Instead, it must assess continuously and adjusted.

Great Cricut Ideas to Bring in Some Cash

By using the innovative design of different Cricut cartridges, you have become an expert. Talk of your colleagues is your creative scrapbooking. Your wonders of creative Cricut concepts are your personalized greeting card collections. Friends say your invention can compete with any card or scrapbook sold in your local stationery store, which commercially manufactures.

So, did you think you would make cash from your incredible and kind of craft? There are excellent ways to make your love cash.

Although there are thousands of craftspeople who like to use their Cricut die cutting machine, the software they don't know how to operate. Take this opportunity to provide your custom order service and to create cut files that can be used by your customers. Craft forums offer you the chance to see what other people want, and then make those cut files, especially on eBay, and sell them on the internet.

Show custom cards in the local arts and crafts shop and invites them to you. It sells to its clients. A customized card or invitation likes for special occasions like a birthday, anniversaries, birthdays, etc. Because of infinite Cricut concepts, your creation can be unlimited and distinctive.

Infinite theme parties for children organized. Parents enjoy celebrating their child's birthday with topics such as a Disney costume feast or a Pokémon party. By creating decoration packages for such events, you can easily make some money. Print and cut off a variety of décors, make custom names or play cards for children, even after the party, to collect and trade with each other.

As scrapbooks become more popular every day, scrapbook enthusiasts will sell them using the Cricut machine to cut scrapbooks' page layout. You will undoubtedly have lots of designs and thoughts, as passionate as you are about scrapbooking.

Did you know that you can also sell your ideas to interior designers or homeowners who love home decoration? You can spread your money to home shops, wallpapers, and paint stores and leave them with your business cards or flyers to publicize your wall art services. Interior decorators can also recruit your services if you show them your home decoration projects. You can use the Design Studio and the Vinyl Sheets to create any design, art words, character cartoons, or symbols you have made.

With your endless Cricut ideas, you can make additional money using Cricut software and technological innovation with your skills and experience while continuing your passion for creating beautiful crafts for everybody to enjoy for years.

CHAPTER 3: IS IT POSSIBLE TO BUILD A BUSINESS WITH THE CRICUT MACHINE? HOW?

Setting Up Your Cricut Business

Setting Up a Website

This is a very important step in the right direction, and here's how you can go about it:

1. **Choose a domain name/URL**

This is very important because this is what your audience or customers will know you by, and everything you create and post will be linked to this domain name. Usually, you can pick one that depicts your brand and what you do. It must be short and easy to remember as well.

2. **Register your domain name/URL**

This can be done with little cash, usually per annum, and helps link your domain name to your hosting service. I would recommend using GoDaddy for domain and hosting services.

3. **Choosing a hosting service**

You will need a hosting service to host your website, and depending on their customer service, reliability, speed, storage space, among others, you can choose one that is very good.

4. **Connect your domain name to your web host**

Some web hosts will not need this step as they offer domain names with their hosting service. However, for those that don't, you will have to connect your domain name by plugging your server name/DNS into your domain name registrar account.

5. **Install WordPress**

WordPress is an application that allows you to manage and work on your website, and it is absolutely free, straight forward and consumer friendly.

6. **Choose a theme for your website**

Get one that suits your brand, content and services. You can get them free or subscribe for Premium ones at a price.

7. **Configure your website**

Now that you've got a functional website with a theme to it, you may want to configure your website. You will want to organize the information you give about what you do and what you have to offer, add one or more colors and make it easy for visitors to navigate through your site.

8. **Add content**

Get all yourself out there by uploading, writing and posting what you have to offer on your website. Something that will appeal to your customers and leave them satisfied.

If setting up your website is something you know you may not be able to do on your own, you can employ the service of a web developer to create your website. This will help you focus on making money with your Cricut by creating more designs.

Advertising

Common ways of advertising as a new service provider include:

- Social media ads on Instagram, Pinterest, Facebook and other social media sites.
- Video Ads on blogs, YouTube, etc.
- Digital display ads
- Magazines and newspapers
- Direct mail and personal sales

Other means are:

- Outdoor Advertising
- Radio and Podcasts
- Product Placement on Television shows and YouTube channels.

- Email marketing.
- Event marketing.

Taking Orders and Shipping

Customers can place orders via email or contact phone numbers that you place on your website. It could be daily or within specified time limits or days, depending on how well you can deliver. Ensure you get all necessary arrangements in place before taking orders from areas far from your reach so as to prevent disappointments and delays thus, ruining your reputation as a service provider. Shipping arrangements depend on your location and the taxes involved.

Saving money using your Cricut Explore machine for business. You can employ the services of any bank or saving institutions around you to build your financial strength as well as grow your wealth.

Note:
1. If you took a loan, ensure you pay off your debt.
2. On your first batch of sales, take out your capital to continue business and save profit.

CHAPTER 4: BEGINNER PROJECTS WITH THE CRICUT EXPLORE AIR 2

How to Make Simple Handmade Cards

If you want to test your crafting skills, the Cricut Explore Air 2 has made it possible for you to be creative with designing whatever you want to design on the Design Space. We will be teaching you how to use your Cricut Explore Air 2 to make simple cards.

1. Log into Design Space with your details. Do this on your Mac/Windows PC.
2. On the left-hand side of the screen, select "Shapes". Add the square shape.
3. By default, there is no rectangular shape, so you have to make do with the square shape. However, you can adjust the length and width. You can change the shape by clicking on the padlock icon at the bottom left of the screen. Change the size and click on the padlock icon to relock it.
4. Click "Score Line" and align.
5. Create your first line. It's advisable you make it long. Use the "zoom in" option for better seeing if you are having difficulties with sight.
6. Select the first line you have created and duplicate. It's easier that way than creating another long line. You will see the duplicate option when you right-click on your first line.
7. Follow the same duplication process and create a third line.
8. Rotate the third line to the bottom so that it connects the other two parallel lines you earlier created. Remember to zoom in to actually confirm the lines are touching.
9. Duplicate another line, just like you did the other. Rotate it to the top so that it touches the two vertical parallel lines. You should have created a big rectangular shape.
10. Highlight your rectangular shape (card). Select "Group" at the upper right corner.
11. Now, change the "Score" option "cut". You can do this by clicking on the little pen icon.
12. Your lines will change from dotted to thick straight lines.

13. Select the "Attach" option at the bottom right-hand side of the screen. The four lines will be attached and will get the card ready to be cut on the mat correctly.
14. You can adjust the size of the card as you like. At this point, you can add images or texts to beautify your card anyhow you want it.
15. After you are done, select the "Make it" button and then "Continue" to cut your card out.

If you don't know how to create a style on your cards with shapes, follow these simple steps to create one.

1. Select your choice of shape. Let's choose stars, for example. Select the "Shape" option and click on the star.
2. Add two stars.
3. Select the first star and click "Flip" and then select "Flip Vertical".
4. Align both stars to overlap them at the center.
5. Select "Weld" to make a new shape and add a score line.
6. Align them at the center and attach them.
7. Select "Make it button" and then "Continue" to cut your card out.

If you don't know how to add text or write on a card, follow the processes below.

1. Select your choice of shape. Let's choose a hexagon, for example. Select the "Shape" option and click on the hexagon shape.
2. Use your favorite pattern.
3. Add a scoring line and rotate it.
4. Click "Add Text". A box will appear on the canvas or work area of your project. Write your desired text. Let's say you choose to write "A Star Is Born Strong" and "And Rugged" on the two hexagonal shapes. Choose the fonts and style of writing.
5. Select the first text and flip vertically or horizontally.

6. Select the second text and flip vertically. Click "Flip" and select flip vertically. Doing this will make the text not look upside down.
7. Attach Select "Make it button" and then "Continue" to cut your card out. Follow the cutting process on the screen to full effect.

Simple T-Shirt

In this tutorial, we will be using iron-on vinyl. Iron-on vinyl is a type of vinyl, like an adhesive that will stick to any fabric when applied using an iron.

1. Log into your Design Space.
2. Select "New Project" and then click on "Templates" in the top left corner. Choosing a template makes it easier to visualize your design to know how good or bad it will be on your T-shirt.
3. Choose "Classic T-Shirt" and pick your preferred style, size, and color.
4. You will see tons of beautiful designs for iron-on T-shirts. Browse through the entire images before you make your choice.
5. Remember, if your preferred design isn't available, you can upload your pictures to the Cricut Design Space. We have created a tutorial on how to upload your own images to Cricut Design Space.
6. After you have selected the image, resize the image to fit the T-shirt. You can do this by clicking the resize handle in the bottom part of your design and dragging the mouse to enlarge or reduce.
7. When you are done, click the "Make it" button in the top right corner. You will be told to connect your Cricut machine.
8. Toggle the green "Mirror" button on. Toggling it on will make sure your design is not cut backward.
9. Face the shiny part of your vinyl design down on your cutting mat. Remember to move the smart set dial to the iron-on option.

10. Remove all the vinyl designs you don't want to be transferred to your project when it's ironed. Use your weeding tool to remove those little bits that will jeopardize your beautiful design. This process is called weeding.
11. Transfer your design to your T-shirt when you are done weeding. You can either use an iron or an EasyPress. Preheat your EasyPress before use.

Basswood Quote with Vinyl Highlights

Here's what you'll need for this project:
- Transfer tape
- One sheet of vinyl in the color and finish of your choosing
- A plate of basswood, balsa wood, or a chipboard

And that's it!

Here's how to make your first beautiful project with Cricut. First, you will choose and design a quote. Open a worksheet (a Canvas) in Design Space and set it up to present the size of your text box or a quote that's going to be cut. You can choose a phrase from the software's library, or you can open a text box and write one on your own. Next, position the text box on the Canvas and adjust font, style, and size.

The designing process is now over, and all you need to figure out is whether you wish to cover the entire quote with vinyl or use it only in certain layers (lines or parts of lines) to create highlights or accents. If you're confident in your layering skills, you can first start by cutting the quote on your wooden plate and then go back to edit the project. Now, you'll choose only certain layers (lines) to cut from vinyl.

If you don't wish to do the project this way, you can instead cut an entire phrase in vinyl and apply it to the wood. You'll do this simply by keeping the design and changing the material settings. If you don't want to cover the whole quote with vinyl, you can select only certain letters (e.g., first and last, or every other) to still have some contrast with your design.

Finally, print the vinyl layers.

Once you've cut both wood and vinyl, it's time to transfer the vinyl design. Use transfer tape to lift the cut-out from the vinyl sheet and apply it to the designated spot on your wooden cut-out. Repeat this process until you've set all the pieces into place and your wonderful design is finished.

A Flower Corsage

Whether for prom or Mother's Day, this project can be made in five easy steps and be a great present for a loved one in your family. If you're making a corsage for prom, make sure to match the colors of the flower to the colors of the dress. When you look at the picture, the design may appear to be more complex than it actually is. Don't let this intimidate you; the steps for making this project are easy and simple. The more time you spend making corsage flowers, the easier it will get. Plus, these are reusable and will last you multiple years.

For this project, you'll need cardstock, ribbons, pins, scissors, and glue. Let's go over the basic steps for the project:

1. Choose a flower template, and print it onto the cardstock.
2. Spray the cardstock, and curl the paper into the shapes you'd like. Adding moisture to the paper will help you create the desired shape.

3. Start gluing the flower together. Join tabs of each section, add leaves, and let the flower dry. To further set and secure the flower, use a clothespin to hold the flower's ends together while they're drying.
4. If you want to make your flower more colorful, add some color using markers or watercolors. Finally, glue the remaining parts of the flower together and let it dry.
5. Next, start making the ribbon. Cut a piece of ribbon in the desired length, and glue it to the flower once it's fully dry. You can further secure it with a pin.

If you have young children, you can make a Cricut corsage as a family project. You could involve the children in painting and gluing the flower and, depending on their age, you can also let them choose and cut ribbons.

CHAPTER 5: BEGINNER PROJECTS WITH CRICUT MAKER

Shamrock Earrings

Materials:
- Cricut Maker
- Earring (from a Cricut Project)
- Rotary Wheel
- Knife Blade
- FabricGrip Mat
- StrongGrip Mat
- Weeder Tool
- Cricut Leather
- Scraper Tool

- Adhesive
- Pebbled-Faux Leather
- Earring Hooks

Instructions:
1. First, open the Cricut Project (Earring). You can now either click on "Make It" or "Customize" to edit it.
2. Once you've selected one, click on "Continue."
3. Immediately the Cut page pops up, select your material and wait for the "Load" tools and Mat to appear.
4. Make your Knife blade your cutting tool in clamp B. This will be used on the leather.
5. On the StrongGrip mat, place the leather and make sure it's facing down. Then load the mat into the machine and tap the "Cut" flashing button.
6. When the scoring has been done, go back to the cutting tool and change it to a rotary wheel so that you can use it on the Faux leather.
7. Similarly, place your Faux leather on your FabricGrip Mat, facing down. Then load the mat into the machine and tap the "Cut" flashing button.
8. Take away all the items on the mat with your scraper tool. Be careful with the small fringes, though.
9. Make a hole in the top circle by making use of the weeder tool. Make sure the hole is large enough to make the earring hooks fit in.
10. If necessary, you may have to twist the hook's end with the pliers to fit them in.
11. Close them up after you have looped them inside the hole that was made inside the earring.
12. Finally, you should glue the Shamrock to the surface of the earring with adhesive. Wait for it to dry before using it.

Valentine's Day Classroom Cards

Materials:
- Cricut Maker
- Card Designs (Write Stuff Coloring)
- Cricut Design Space
- Dual Scoring Wheel
- Pens
- Cardstock
- Crayons
- Shimmer Paper

Instructions:
1. Open the card designs (write stuff coloring) on the Design Space, and then click on "Make it" or "Customize" to make edits.
2. When all the changes have been done, Cricut will request you to select a material. Select cardstock for the cards and shimmer paper for the envelopes.
3. Cricut will send you a notification when you need to change the pen colors while creating the card, and then it will start carving the card out automatically.
4. You will be prompted later on to change the blade because of the double scoring wheel. It is advisable to use the double scoring wheel with shimmer paper; they both work best together.
5. When the scoring has been finished, replace the scoring wheel with the previous blade.
6. After that, fold the flaps at the score lines in the direction of the paper's white side, and then attach the side tabs to the exterior of the bottom tab by gluing them together.
7. You may now write "From:" and "To:" before placing the crayons into the slots.
8. Place the cards inside the envelopes and tag them with a sharp object.

Cricut Burlap Wreaths

Now, let's make a simple, neutral-looking burlap wreath that you can decorate with themed pins, badges, or stickers whenever you want to change up your decoration. You'll make a base for the burlap wreath on your Cricut, after which you can add holiday or season-themed decorations. If you're looking to commercialize your Cricut craft, you can easily create the burlap, add a couple of sets of embellishments for different seasons and holidays, and sell your product.

For this project, you should first choose the desired theme and the color scheme of your decoration. Keep in mind that burlap will be the best cut on the Cricut Maker, but you can choose an alternative material for your Explore or Joy. You should also choose the style of embellishments you wish to use, which you can get from any store.

To further embellish your wreath, you can use different types of colored paper and cut them into various shapes such as snowflakes, leaves, hearts, or flowers—the choice is all yours.

Now, let's start making your all-in-on burlap Cricut wreath, shall we? Here's what you'll need for your project:

1. A wreath, which you can get made from foam, straw, or even cardstock.
2. One burlap ribbon. If you wish to switch the style and embellishments of your wreath, I recommend choosing a neutral-colored ribbon. Beige, gray, brown, or even deep red, green, or powder-rose will work. If you want the wreath to be an accent piece, you can also choose a silver or a golden ribbon. These are also neutral, will work with most of the embellishments, and should flatter a variety of wall paints and interior styles. The color of the burlap should also complement your interior design and contrast the color of your walls.
3. Printable embellishments. For this project, you can choose to focus on a single theme or cut multiple themed embellishments from the start. I recommend looking for basic, neutral shapes and designs that are premade in your Design Space, cutting a few for testing purposes, and then choosing the ones that work best with your paper and burlap.
4. Sewing pins
5. Glue

Now, let's start making your burlap wreath. First, wrap the burlap around the wreath base and set it with glue and/or pins.

Start printing and cutting your embellishments. Given that you'll use a larger number of smaller embellishments, you can either design each individual embellishments or find a suitable printable pattern, print it, and cut out the desired shapes manually.

Attach the embellishments to the ribbon of your wreath, and you're done. As you can see, the larger portion of this project consists of printing and cutting your embellishments. The very basic way to do this project would be to just cut interesting shapes out of colored paper, metallic paper, crepe paper, or any other type of paper that works with the style you choose.

If you wish to add complexity and quality to your project, you can first write notes or draw pictures on the desired shapes and even apply some embossing or scoring to add flair and texture. It all depends on the machine you have, your style, taste, and, of course, creativity.

Personalized Pillows

Personalized pillows are another fun idea and are incredibly easy to make. To begin, you open up Design Space and choose a new project. From here, select the icon at the bottom of the screen itself, choosing your font. Type the words you want and drag the text as needed to make it bigger. You can also upload images if you want to create a huge picture on the pillow itself.

From here, you want to press the attach button for each box, so that they work together and both are figured when centered, as well. You then press make it – and you want to turn to mirror on, since this will, again, be on iron-on vinyl. From here, you load the iron-on vinyl with the shiny side down, the press continues, follow the prompts, and make sure it's not jammed in, either. Let the machine work its magic with cutting and from there, you can press the weeding tool to get the middle areas out.

Set your temperature on the easy press for the right settings, and then push it onto the material, ironing it on and letting it sit for 10 to 15 seconds. Let it cool, and then take the transfer sheet off. There you have it! A simple pillow that works wonders for your crafting needs.

Cards!

Finally, cards are a great project idea for Cricut makers. They're simple, and you can do the entire project with cardstock. To make this, you first want to open up Design Space, and from there, put your design in. If you like images of ice cream, then use that. If you want to make Christmas cards, you can do that, too. Basically, you can design whatever you want to on this.

Now, you'll then want to add the text. You can choose the font that you want to use, and from there, write out the message on the card, such as "Merry Christmas." At this point, instead of choosing to cut, you want to choose the right option – the make it option. You don't have to mirror this, but check that your design fits properly on the cardstock itself. When choosing material for writing, make sure you choose the cardstock.

From there, insert your cardstock into the machine, and then, when ready, you can press go, and the Cricut machine will design your card. This may take a minute, but once it's done, you'll have a wonderful card in place. It's super easy to use. Cricut cards are a great personalized way to express yourself, creating a one-of-a-kind, sentimental piece for you to gift to friends and family.

Printable Stickers

Printable stickers are the next project. This is super simple and fun for parents and kids. The Explore Air 2 machine works best. With this one, you want the print then cut feature, since it makes it much easier. To begin, go to Design Space and download images of ice cream or whatever you want, or upload images of your own. You click on a new project, and on the left side that says images, you can choose the ones you like and insert more of these on there. From here, choose the image and flatten it, since this will make it into one piece rather than just a separate file for each. Resize as needed to make sure that they fit where you're putting them.

You can copy/paste each element until you're done. Once ready, press saves, and then choose this as a print, then cut the image. Click the big button at the bottom that says make it. Make sure everything is good, then press continue, and from there, you can load the sticker paper into the machine. Make sure to adjust this to the right setting, which for sticker paper is the vinyl set. Put the paper into there and load them in, and when ready, the press goes – it will then cut the stickers as needed.

From there, take them out and decorate. You can use ice cream or whatever sticker image you want!

CHAPTER 6: ADVANCED PROJECTS WITH THE CRICUT EXPLORE AIR 2

How to Make a Leather Bracelet

The Cricut Explore Air 2 can be pretty amazing in doing a variety of things. One of those things is being able to make a leather bracelet with your Cricut. You can make pretty cool designs that you can turn into wearable pieces of jewelry. To make a leather bracelet, you need your Cricut Explore Air 2, a deep point blade, faux leather, marker, ruler, craft knife, bracelet cut file, transfer tape, and a grip mat. You will also need glue, an EasyPress or iron, and an SVG design to crown it up.

Follow these steps to create your leather bracelets.

1. Log into your Design Space account menu.
2. Select "Canvas".
3. Upload an art set from Jen Goode into the Design Space. The Jen Goode is a set of designs with 4 different image layouts.
4. Ungroup the designs and hide the layers you don't require after selecting your design.
5. Create a base cut of the shape you want to use. Use a cut file and create the shape you want. For example, you can use a shape tool to create a circular design.
6. Add circle cutouts with basic shapes. Duplicate the layer so that you will use it for the back of the bracelet.
7. Set your iron or EasyPress ready and apply the vinyl to the uppermost layer of your leather.
8. Spread a thin coat of glue on the back of the duplicated layer and press it with the other layer together.
9. Add your bracelet strap or chain together with some other ornaments.
10. Congratulations! You have just made your first leather bracelet.

Making a Stencil for Painting with the Cricut Explore Air 2

To make a stencil, you can either use the ready-made designs or make your own design. This tutorial will be based on how to create a stencil for painting.

1. Log in to your Design Space.
2. Click "Canvas" from the drop-down menu.
3. Click "Add Text".
4. Highlight text and change to your preferred font.
5. All your letters must be separated. If they aren't, click the ungroup button to separate. The letters must overlap. This will allow you to drag each letter as you please.
6. Arrange your text line as you want it. If you notice each letter is still showing individually, highlight the text box and click "Weld" at the bottom right of the panel.
7. Click "Attach". Make sure the text is highlighted. This will make the letters arranged properly when it goes to the cut mat.
8. Your stencil design is ready!

Making a Vinyl Sticker

First of all, you need to have an idea of the vinyl sticker that you want. Get ideas online or from forums. Once you have gotten the picture, make a sketch of it to see how the sticker would look. After you have done this, follow the steps below;

1. Use an image editing software like Photoshop or Illustrator. Design to your taste and save. Make sure you know the folder it is saved to.
2. Now, open your Design Space.
3. Click "New Project".
4. Scroll to the bottom left-hand side and click "Upload".
5. Drag and drop the design you created with your photo editing app.
6. Select your image type. If you want to keep your design simple, select simple.
7. Select which area of the image is not part of it.

8. Before you forge ahead, select the image as cut to have a preview. You can go back if there is a need for adjustments.
9. Select "Cut".
10. Weed excess vinyl.
11. Use a transfer tape on top of the vinyl. This will make the vinyl stay in position.
12. Go over the tape and ensure all the bibles are nowhere to be found.
13. Peel away the transfer tape, and you have your vinyl sticker.

Giant Vinyl Stencils

Vinyl stencils are a good thing to create, too, but they can be hard. Big vinyl stencils make for an excellent Cricut project, and you can use them in various places, including bedrooms for kids. You only need the explore Air 2, the vinyl that works for it, a pallet, sander and, of course, paint and brushes. The first step is preparing the pallet for painting or whatever surface you plan on using this for. From here, you create the mermaid tail (or any other large image) in Design Space. Now, you'll learn immediately that big pieces are hard to cut and impossible to do all at once in Design Space.

What you need to do is section each design accordingly and remove any middle pieces. Next, you can add square shapes to the image, slicing it into pieces so that it can be cut on a cutting mat that fits. At this point, you cut out the design by pressing make it, choosing your material, and working in sections.

From here, you put it on the surface that you're using, piecing this together with each line, and you should have one image after piecing it all together. Then, draw out the line on vinyl and then paint the initial design. For the second set of stencils, you can simply trace the first one and then paint the inside of them. At this point, you should have the design finished. When done, remove it very carefully. And there you have it! Bigger stencils can be a bit of a project since it involves trying to use multiple designs all at once, but with the right care and the right designs, you'll be able to create whatever it is you need to in Design Space so you can get the results you're looking for.

Cricut Quilts

Quilts are a bit hard to do for many people, but did you know that you can use Cricut to make it easier? Here, you'll learn an awesome project that will help you do this. To begin, you start with the Cricut Design Space. Here, you can add different designs that work for your project. For example, if you're making a baby blanket or quilt with animals on it, you can add little fonts with the names of the animals, or different pictures of them, too. From here, you want to make sure you choose the option to reverse the design. That way, you'll have it printed on correctly. At this point, make your quilt. Do various designs and sew the quilt as you want to.

From here, you should cut it on the iron-on heat transfer vinyl. You can choose that, and then press cut. The image will then cut into the piece. At this point, it'll cut itself out, and you can proceed to transfer this with some parchment paper. Use an EasyPress for best results and push it down. There you go, an easy addition that will definitely enhance the way your blankets look.

Cricut Unicorn Backpack

If you're making a present for a child, why not give them some cool unicorns? Here is a lovely unicorn backpack you can try to make. To make this, you need ¾ yards of a woven fabric – something that's strong, since it will help with stabilizing the backpack. You'll also need half a yard of quilting cotton for the lining. The coordinating fabric should be around about an eighth of a yard. You'll need about a yard of fusible interfacing, some strap adjuster rings, a zipper that's about 14 inches and doesn't separate, and some stuffing for the horn.

To start, you'll want to cut the main fabric, and you should use straps, the loops, a handle, some gussets for a zipper, and the bottom and side gussets. The lining should be done, too, and you should make sure you have the interfacing. You can use fusible flex foam, too, to help make it a little bit bulkier.

From here, cut everything and then apply the interfacing to the backside, and the flex foam should be adjusted to achieve the bulkiness you are looking for. You can trim this, too. The interfacing should be one on the backside and then add the flex foam to the main fabric. The adhesive side of this will be on the right-hand side of the interfacing.

Fold the strap pieces in half and push one down on each backside. Halve it, and then press it again, and stitch these closer to every edge, and also along the short-pressed edge, as well. From here, do the same thing with the other side, but add the ring for adjustment, and stitch the bottom of these to the main part of the back piece. Then add them both to the bottom. At this point, you have the earpieces that you should do the backside facing out. Stitch, then flip out and add the pieces. Add these inner pieces to the outer ear, and then stitch these together.

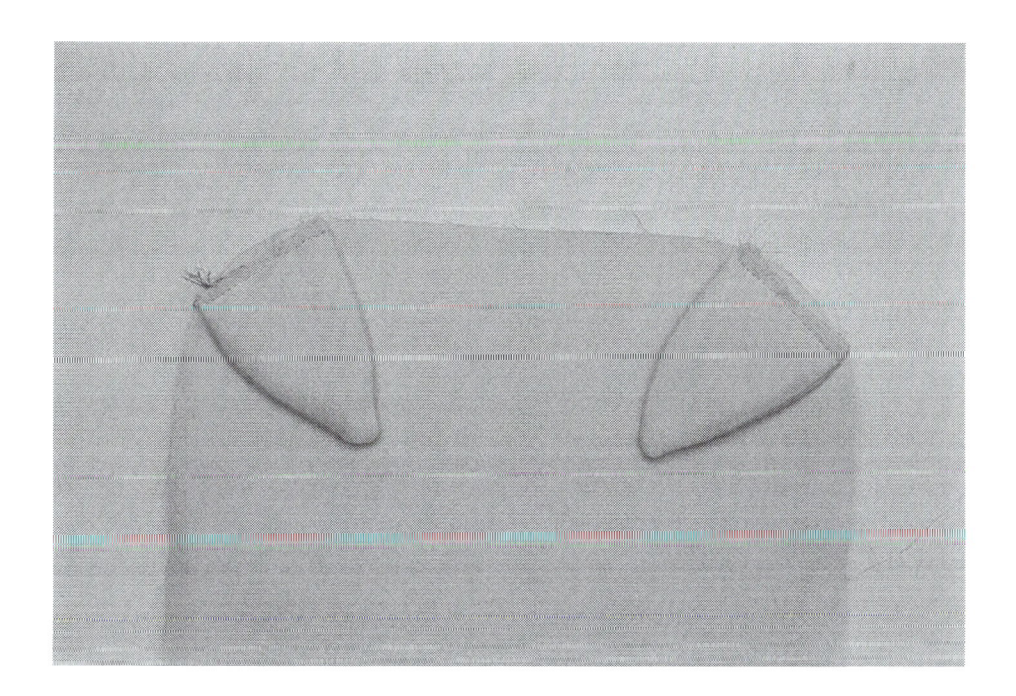

At this point, you make the unicorn face in the Design Space. You'll notice immediately when you use this program everything will be black, but you can change this by adjusting the desired layers to each color. You can also just use a template that fits, but you should always mirror this before you cut it.

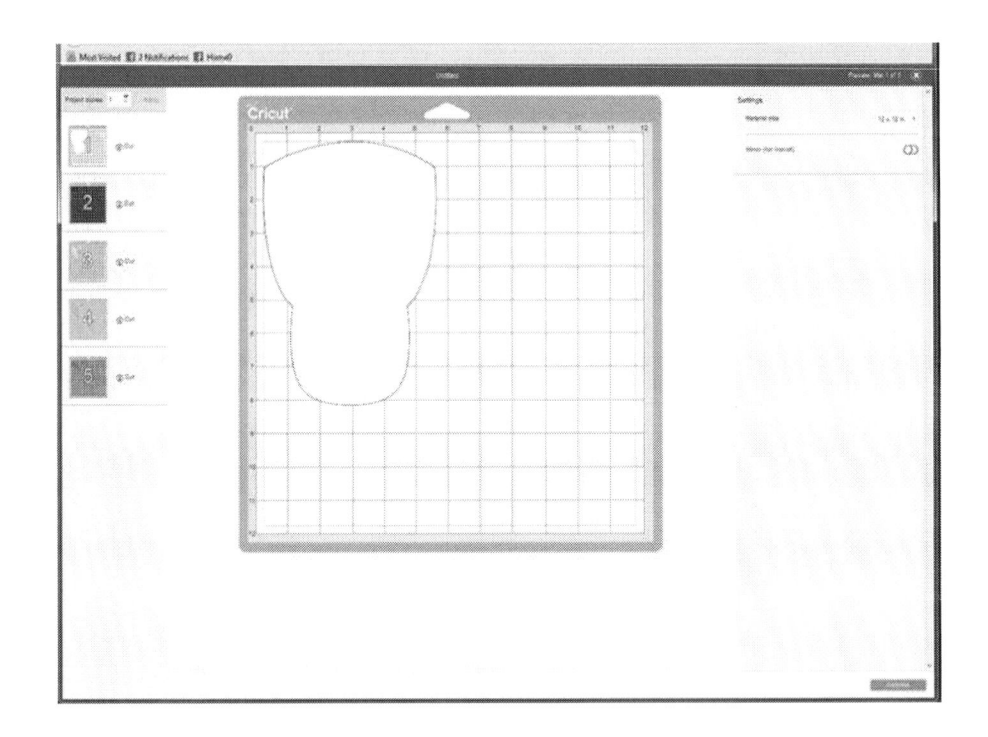

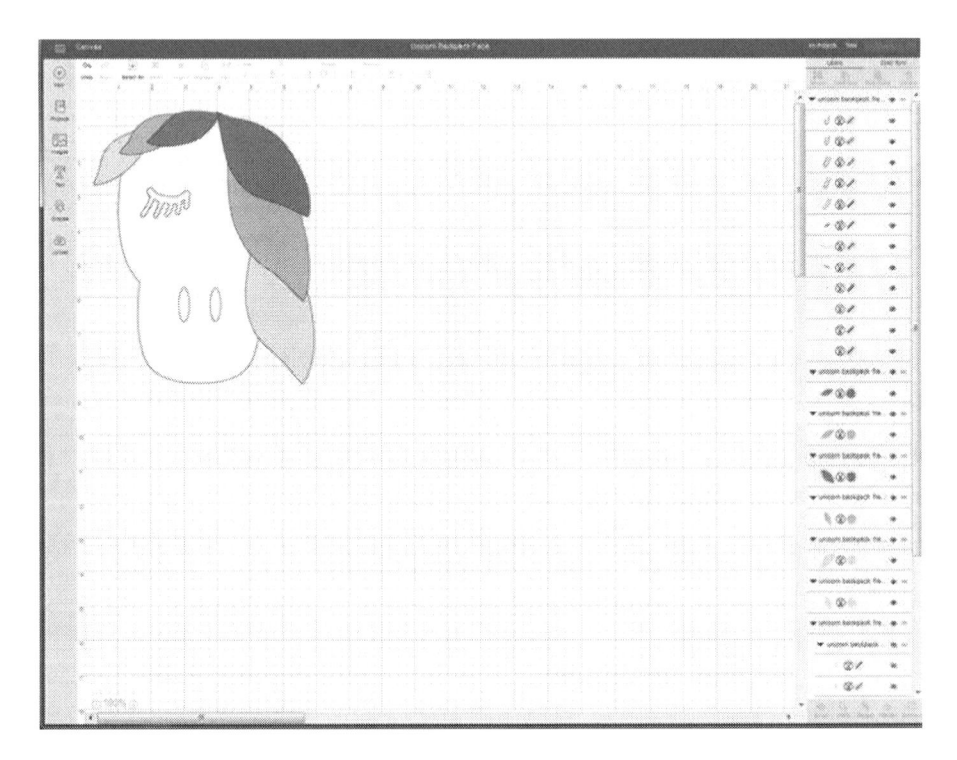

Choose vinyl, and then insert the material onto the cutting mat. From there, cut it and remove the iron-on slowly.

You will need to do this in pieces, which is fine because it allows you to use different colors. Remember to insert the right color for each cut. At this point, add the zipper, and there you go!

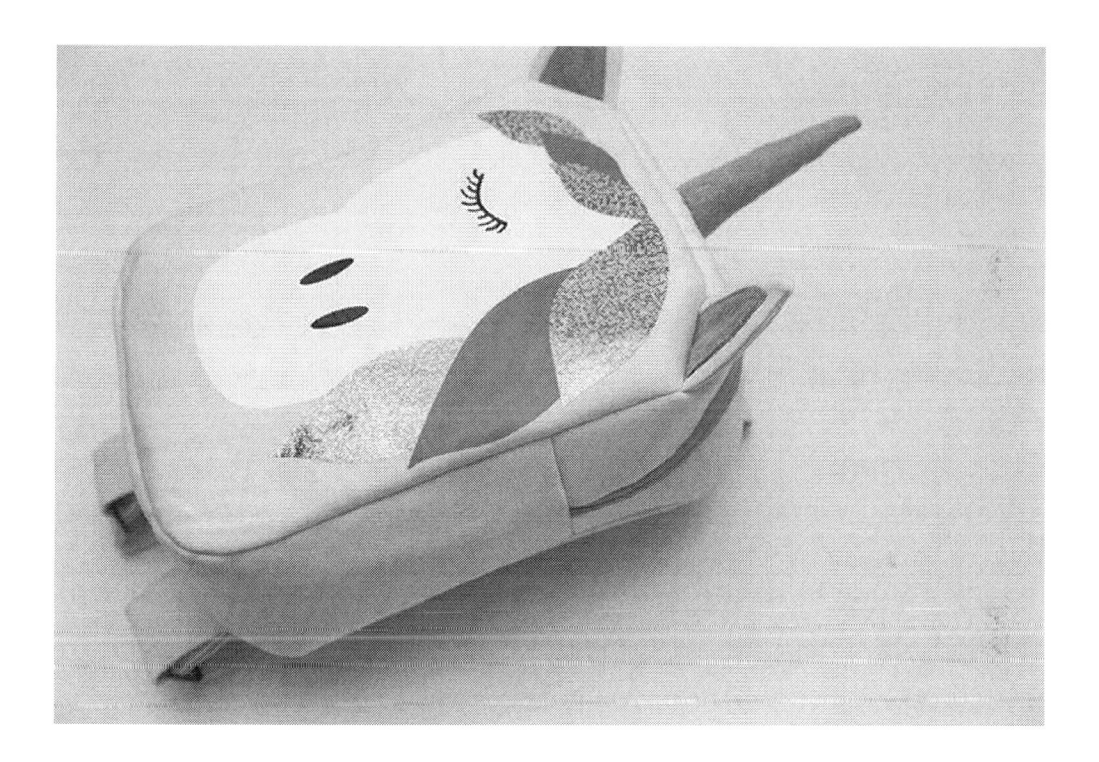

Diamond Planters

Finally, we have some diamond planters. These are a bit complicated, but there is a pattern to do it. Essentially, you create the diamond design and the trapezoids on top and then cut them into the chipboard. Make sure to choose a chipboard in your materials. From there, cut them, and then use masking tape to hold these pieces as you glue. When done, you essentially do the same with the trapezoid pieces and put them on top. Then, just get the outside seams. Once dried, remove the tape. This project is more complicated due to the extra steps you need to take with assembling it and getting the Cricut measurements right.

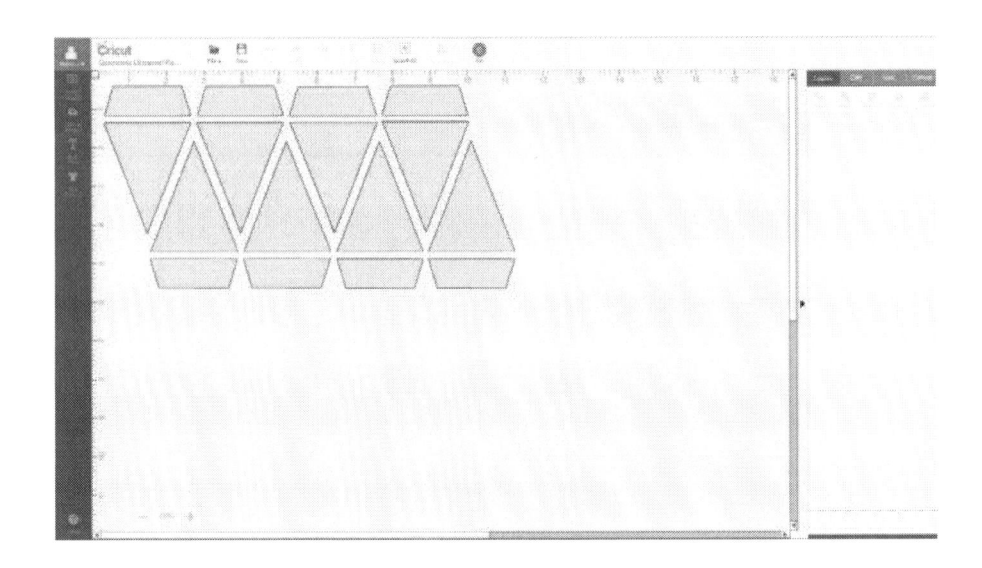

Cricut projects are fun, and with the instructions in this section of the book, you should have everything you need to get started with some of the easier, more popular projects. There are tons more out there to choose from, so once you've got a handle on the ones we've suggested, take a look and see what else you might be interested in creating. Your options are almost limitless, thanks to your Cricut machine.

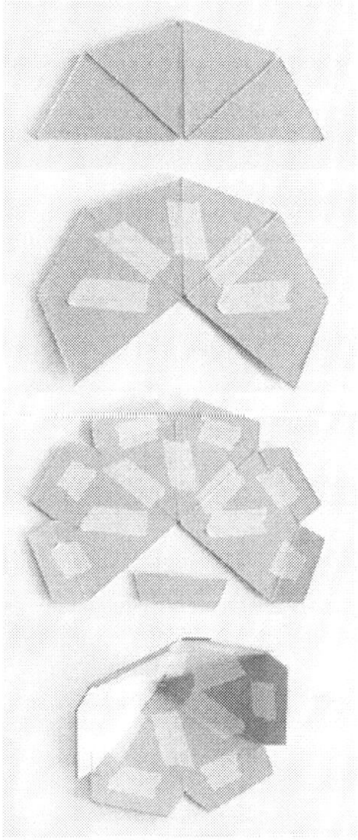

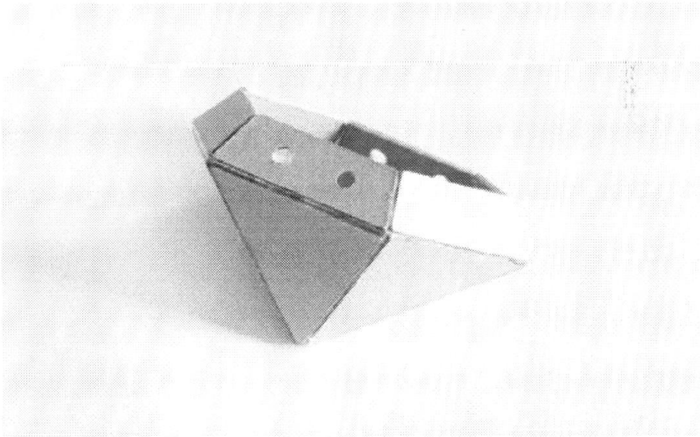

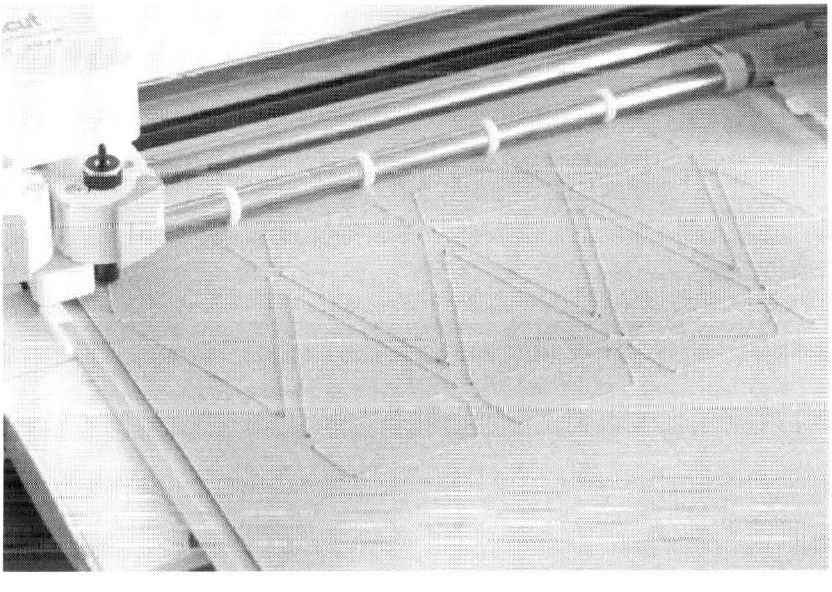

CHAPTER 7: ADVANCED PROJECTS WITH THE CRICUT MAKER

Is there truly a complex project with Cricut? After spending some time working with the machine, I realized that it's only the result that may come across as difficult. Essentially, Cricut's functions are vital to understand. Advanced skills pretty much include learning how to combine them in a smart, creative way to achieve what appears to be unachievable. Of course, careful planning is necessary for your craftwork to turn out the way you want.

A Large 3D Cricut Shadowbox

How about making a 3D lighted shadow box? These projects might look difficult to create, but it's far easier than you might think. When making this design, you will apply the technique known as layering. Essentially, you will choose an image or a figure, then cut it in such a way as to separate layers of lines and elements to create depth.

For this project, you'll need:

- Three to five paper sheets
- A lightbox
- Hot glue
- A sheet of craft foam

Now, let's start making your 3D box. Here are the steps that you need to follow:

1. The first step is to create your design in Design Space. Start by making a square shape in the size of your shadowbox. This will be the frame for your drawing. Build the image from the back to forward in layers, which creates the 3D effect.

2. When making your drawing, first add the background, then the furthest elements of the drawing, like houses, trees, etc. Finally, apply the last layer, which contains the elements of the drawing that are the closest to the eye. This form of layering creates an illusion of depth in the cut after you apply one sheet of paper over the other. However, each of the elements should touch the surface of the square; the layers shouldn't overlap.
3. Measure the inside of your box to double-check the dimensions and click "Make it". You will cut the layers sheet by sheet, starting from the final layer and moving toward the first one on your design. Since you'll be cutting a complex image, some of the smaller pieces of paper might get stuck to the mat. Make sure to remove them regularly before starting a second cut. Also, look at the images on your Design Space frequently to remind yourself of what each layer is supposed to look like. Since you're not printing a complex drawing on a single sheet of paper but instead creating a complex image out of multiple sheets of paper, you might get lost in all the shapes and lines.
4. Now that you've cut all the layers, cut thin strips of craft foam to create the "spacers" for your project. You will create a type of foam frame for each of the layers, which separate one from the next. Make sure that the foam is at the edge of your paper, and glue the foam strips over the four back edges of your sheet. This means gluing while the paper is turned upside-down. Repeat these steps on all layers of paper, and apply each of them right-side-up, one on top of the other, into the box and over the lights. Once you're finished layering, apply the lid. The lid will keep the layers fixed.

If you followed all of the steps, you now have a whimsical-looking shadow box that will look wonderful in your or your child's bedroom. I advise getting a high-quality lightbox, because disassembling the entire piece if the lights break down might damage the design, aside from being a real hassle. If you don't want to purchase a lightbox, you can use a thick, deeper picture frame you already have and only get adhesive lights. Fix the lights to the inner edges of the frame, and you're finished. In this case, make sure to drill a hole in the bottom corner of the frame for the cord to pass through.

Engraved Jewelry with Cricut

Let's make an engraved charm bracelet!

For this project, you will be using Cricut's engraving tool. You will purchase jewelry pieces for your bracelet, then use the Cricut to add intricate engravings that will give them extra value. For this project, I recommend investing in a stainless steel charm bracelet. Get a bracelet with multiple plates in different shapes and sizes.

You will need:

- The Cricut engraving tool, which has a sharp point that applies pressure to inscribe words and images into plastic, leather, paper, acrylic, and soft metal materials. It is best used on the Cricut Maker, which features the Adaptive Tool System. This system applies the necessary amount of pressure that's needed for engraving. You will not be able to use this tool on the Cricut Explore Air or the Cricut Joy.
- Stainless steel plates in the desired shape and size

- A design for your engraving
- A chain bracelet
- A pair of pliers

Now, let's start making your engraved charm bracelet. Here are the steps for carrying out this project:

1. Start designing your engravings. This process begins by creating templates for your charms and making sure that you're designing for the unique size of each plate. To start designing your engraved charmed plates, open a new Canvas in your Design Space, upload the desired image, or write the text. If you choose a design with thicker lines, you're going to have to fill it with close-together lines. This way, the tool will create multiple thin lines within the selected spaces to create a filling effect.
2. Choose quotes, text, or images that you wish to apply to your plate, and then apply them onto the base shape of your plates. Pay attention to size, legibility, alignment, and the positioning of your engravings. Take your time with this step, and carefully adjust each image, letter, or pattern, because you won't be able to correct them later on.
3. To engrave both the front and the back, you need to separate the work onto two different mats and center the positioning of the design in the exact place where you'll place the plates for the charm bracelet.
4. Next, lay the plates on the designated spots on the mat, and set them with tape. Don't worry, your engraving tool will work well over the tape and won't compromise the design. Don't forget to set up the machine for engraving and to select the correct material for it to apply the right amount of speed and pressure.
5. Load the mat into the machine, press "Make it" in your Design Space, and watch the beauty unfold!
6. After clicking "Make it", the software will guide you to place the tool in the Maker's carrier.

7. If you wish to engrave both sides off the plate, you're going to have to repeat the process for the other side. This means that you'll need to unload the mat, remove the plates, switch sides, and still make sure that they're fixed in the exact spots as previously.

And that's it. With some careful planning and designing, you have a wonderful, unique bracelet that you can keep for yourself or give to someone you love!

Cricut 3D Decorations

Now, let's make a multilayered cardstock decoration. Cardstock may seem like cheap paper, but if you use it the right way, you can create elegant-looking designs. Layering is a technique that requires more planning and technical skill, but it adds value to your creation. For this project, you'll need multiple sheets of different-colored cardstock paper.

Next, you need to find a 3D layered design that you wish to print. There are plenty of both free and paid designs that you can browse through. The design information will also tell you how many layers there are. You can choose whether to print multiple layers on a single sheet of paper or to enlarge a design and print it over the entire paper sheet.

Here are the steps for making this project:

1. Load your layered design into the Design Space, and open the images on a new Canvas. You'll see all of the layers at the top right corner of the screen. Once you click "group", you'll be able to adjust the size for the entire piece.
2. Next, choose the preferred placement of the design on the mat and ungroup the layers. Click "Make it", and start loading the paper and cutting. You'll have to cut each individual layer, then glue one layer over the other while making sure that you're arranging the layers in the right order.
3. Leave the finished piece to dry, and you're done.

Here are a couple of tips to keep in mind when cutting layered decorations:

- Check material settings. Intricate patterns and shapes may not come out well on thicker materials like cardstock. Make sure to check whether the design mentioned the preferred materials to use. If you like a design that will not work with your desired material, you can somewhat compensate by enlarging the design. This will result in a bigger piece but also a better cutting accuracy.
- Be careful with the glue. The more intricate your design is, the more accuracy you'll need when it comes to gluing. If you're working with paper, utilize paper glue, applying it slowly and gently across the surface of a layer.
- To avoid using too much glue, start applying it from the back of the top layer since top layers are almost always the smallest in size. Finish by gluing the front end of the bottom layer, which is usually the thickest and largest.
- If this is your first time making a layered project, I recommend using a pre-made design to see how the cutting works. After you become used to cutting and making designs like these, you can move on to drawing your designs either on a computer or even by hand, then scanning them for cutting and printing.

You can use this technique to make beautiful Christmas ornaments, jewelry like pendants, earrings, and bracelets, and more. You can even utilize this technique to cut layers of fabrics and create elegant, rustic designs.

CHAPTER 8: PROJECT AND IDEAS WITH VYNIL

Texture Cuts

One of the significant selling purposes of the Maker is the way that it comes outfitted with the plastic new Rotary Blade. On account of a unique floating and moving activity—together with the large 4kg of power behind the Cricut Maker—this implies the machine can cut any texture.

We've generally been compelled to utilize an uncommon texture cutter before, as the work area slicing machines weren't incredible to handle heavier textures. We adore the way that the Maker is an across the board machine. Furthermore, it comes prepared furnished with a texture cutting mat, so you can cut many textures without utilizing any sponsorship. Stunning!

Balsa Wood Cuts

On account of the astounding 4kg of power and the Knife Blade (sold independently), the Cricut Maker can slice through materials up to 2.4 mm thick. That implies thick textures that had recently been beyond reach with the Cricut and Silhouette machines are accessible to us. We can hardly wait to begin cutting wood with it!

Thick Leather Cuts

In a similar vein as point #4, thick cowhide can be cut with the Maker!

Custom made Cards

Paper crafters aren't forgotten about with the Maker either. Paper and card cuts will be simpler and faster than at any other time on account of the power and exactness of the machine. Your handcrafted cards just went up a level…

Jigsaw Puzzles

With the Knife Blade, we realize that the Cricut Maker can slice through a lot of thicker materials than at any other time.

Christmas Tree Ornaments

The Rotary Blade that vows to slice through any texture is the ideal instrument for designing occasion adornments. Scour the sewing design library for Christmassy designs (we have our eye on the gingerbread man decoration!) Cut out the example utilizing felt or whatever texture you want, and afterward sew it together independently.

Blankets

Cricut has collaborated with Riley Blake Designs to offer a variety of knitting designs in the sewing design library. This implies you can utilize the Maker to precisely remove your sewing pieces before sewing them together independently.

Felt Dolls and Soft Toys

One of the Simplicity designs we have our eye on in the sewing design library is the 'felt doll and garments' example. We know a couple of young ladies and young men who'd love a natively constructed doll to add to their accumulation. Just select the example, cut and sew.

Shirt Transfers

The Cricut Maker machine will be a whizz at removing your warmth move vinyl for you to move your designs to texture. You should design your exchange in Design Space, load the creator with your warmth move vinyl (or significantly sparkle HTV on the off chance that you're feeling daring). Instruct the machine to begin cutting, and after that, iron your exchange onto your T-shirt. Otherwise, you could utilize the spic and span Cricut EasyPress to move the vinyl—it's everything the comfort of an iron meets the adequacy of a warmth press!

Doll Clothes

What's more, doll garments as well! Make a gander at in move on these American Girl doll designs.

Texture Appliques

Also, accessible to purchase independently is the reinforced texture edge in lodging, which will enable you to cut increasingly confusing texture designs, similar to applique. In contrast to the sharp revolving edge, the reinforced texture cutting edge requires strong support on the material to cut adequately.

Calligraphy Signs

The Cricut Maker's essential selling point is its Adaptive Tool System. This is the component that will guarantee that you keep your Maker for eternity. It's a device framework that not just fits with every one of the instruments and sharp edges of the Explore family. However, it will provide with every future apparatus and cutting edges made by Cricut as well. Furthermore, one of these apparatuses is the calligraphy pen. Perfect for card making and sign making!

Gems Making

If you like to fiddle with gems making close by your art cutting, you should attempt to consolidate the two sooner or later. The intensity of the Cricut Maker implies that you can cut thicker materials than before that are appropriate to complicated gems designs. And keeping in mind that you aren't probably going to cut gold, silver or precious stone on there at any point soon.

Wedding Invitations and Save the Dates

We as a whole expertise 'little' costs like solicitations and STDs can add to the Uber cost of a wedding. In any case, as producers, we realize how to counterbalance a portion of those expenses by making things like that ourselves. The Cricut Maker is ideal for making excellent solicitations—not exclusively would you be able to remove intricate paper designs, yet that calligraphy pen will prove to be useful once more.

Wedding Menus, Place Cards, and Favor Tags

You're certainly not limited to create before the wedding—you can utilize your Maker to enhance for the huge day itself. The sky is extremely cut off here; however, start with making menus, place cards, and support labels. Attempt and ensure you utilize a comparable design for all your stationery to keep the topic upfront.

Shading Book

Do you know those 'careful shading' books that are extremely popular at present? If you don't need extravagant sprinkling the money for one, why not make your own with the Cricut Maker? All you need is paper, a card, and a breaking design. And after that order the Maker to make your one of a kind, absolutely one of a kind, shading book utilizing the Fine-Point Pen apparatus.

Napkins

Something else we can hardly wait to make with our fresh out of the plastic new Maker is napkins. The world's your shellfish to the extent materials go—anything from calfskin to knit, to metallic sheets and everything in the middle. There are also some incredible napkin designs in the sewing library to look at as well.

Texture Key rings

Something different that grabbed our attention in the sewing design library was a couple of straightforward designs for texture key rings. Once more, the Maker makes it easy—just cut out the example and afterward sew it together.

Headbands and Hair Decorations

Cricut has discharged a machine equipped for trimming through thick calfskin, we are very brave thought for many-sided, steampunk enlivened hair beautifications and even headbands.

Cake Toppers

Do you recollect when Cricut drew out the 'Cake' cutter machine? It was for making shapes made of fondant, gum glue, and so forth. The Maker is anything but a particular cake machine like the Cake is, yet we believe it's merely the machine to make little and complicated paper creates that we can use to finish our cakes with.

Refrigerator Magnets

Much the same as the Cricut Explore machines, the Maker can remove attractive material. Incredible news for magnet gatherers and the extravagant individuals who energizing their icebox!

Window Decals

Extravagant setting up a motivating statement on your windows? Or, on the other hand, maybe an adorable little example on your vehicle's back window? No issue with the Cricut Maker—burden the machine with the window sticker and get making your design.

Scrapbooking Embellishments

We are truly eager to begin utilizing our Maker for embellishments that we can use while scrapbooking. While the Cricut machines have consistently been entirely extraordinary at cutting mind-boggling designs. The magnificently responsive new edges are going to make multifaceted nature a relic of times—notwithstanding when you're cutting fragile materials like tissue paper!

Art Foam Cuts

The Cricut machines have consistently said that they can cut art froth. The Cricut Maker: the 4kg of power implies that this machine can slice through specialty froth like spread, abandoning the Explore machines in the residue.

Boxes and 3D Shapes

Just as having the option to handle all the sewing designs that you can toss at it, the Maker can do all the old school paper makes that we know and love: including having the option to cut 3D shapes and boxes.

Stencils

If your objective with the Maker is to make things that can enable you to make other delightful things, at that point, you're in karma. This is the ideal machine for making stencils with—particularly now as you can utilize thicker materials to make the stencils on, including wood.

Transitory Tattoos

Extravagant a tattoo yet isn't so enthusiastic about the lifetime duty? No stresses: The Maker can draw your design onto tattoo paper—a paper that is covered with exchange film—that you would then be able to use on your body.

Washi Tape

Washi tape is another accessory of the year for scrapbookers. However, it very well may be shockingly costly in case you're purchasing a great deal of it from specialty shops. So, why not make your own? The Cricut Maker can remove washi sheets, enabling you to print and cut your designs on it.

Tended to Envelopes

Maybe when you've completed those handcrafted wedding solicitations we were examining prior, you can proceed onward to the envelopes. As it is, there's no compelling reason to invest the time and vitality tending to them yourself when you have the producer. As it's outfitted with both a Fine-Point and a Calligraphy pen, you'll have the option to address the envelopes naturally. Utilizing whatever vibrant text style you so want.

Dish sets Decals

One of our preferred approaches to try different things with vinyl slicing is to cut designs for the crystal. This is especially cool and viable for when you're facilitating themed gatherings. For example, holding a late spring grill and serving mojitos? Why not beautify tumblers with palm tree decals and coconuts?

Adornments

Also, much the same as you can do with most work area art cutting machines, the Maker makes certain to demonstrate incredible for making general family designs. Regardless of whether that is excellent signage in your storage rooms, adorable patterns in your parlor, or 3D tapestries, you'll have the option to make it with the Cricut Maker.

Pad Transfers

The snappiest method to light up an exhausting pad or pad is to include one of your handcrafted designs in it. Numerous individuals will utilize warmth move vinyl on their fresh out of the box new Maker machine to do precisely that. Our preferred vinyl variant for pads is the rushed iron-on vinyl that gives that delightful finished feel.

3D Bouquet

The truth is out—we're back on the wedding subject once more! This is an incredible method to include a dash of home creating to your wedding—or, far better, to add a few blooms to your home without stressing over their inescapable demise. The Maker is expertly prepared for intricate paper artworks because of its instinctive devices, similar to the Fine-Point sharp edge and scoring stylus.

Present Tags

Present labels are another of those irritating costs that rapidly include after some time— especially during the Christmas season. Be that as it may, with a Cricut, you never need to purchase those tasteless labels again—basically, make your own! Include cardstock.

CHAPTER 9: PROJECT AND IDEAS WITH PAPER

It is ideal to start your first project using paper-based designs, since these projects are easier to not only design but also to cut, regardless of the kind of "Cricut" cutting machine being used. You can get professional-looking results without investing a whole lot of time and money. You will learn to create a variety of projects that you can further customize as you follow the instructions below and have unique designs of your own.

Recipe Stickers

Materials needed – "Cricut" cutting machine, sticker paper, and cutting mat.

Step 1

Use your "Cricut ID" to log in to the "Design Space" application. Then click on the "New Project" button on the top right corner of the screen to start a new project and view a blank canvas.

Step 2

Click on the "Images" icon on the "Design Panel" and type in "recipe stickers" in the search bar. Select the image that works for you, then click on the "Insert Images" button at the bottom of the screen, as shown in the picture below.

Step 3

The image that you have selected will appear on the canvas and can be edited to your preference. You will be able to make all kinds of changes, for example, changing the color and size of the image (sticker should be between 2-4 inches wide). The image selected for this project has the words "stickers" inside the design, so let's delete that by first clicking on the "Ungroup" button and selecting the "Stickers" layer and clicking on the red "x" button. Click on the "Text" button and add the name of your recipe, as shown in the picture below.

Step 4

Now, move the text to the middle of the design and select the entire design, including the text. Then click on "Align" and select "Center Horizontally" and "Center Vertically" so that your text will be uniformly aligned right in the center of the design.

Step 5

Select all the layers of the design and click on the "Group" icon on the top right of the screen under "Layers Panel." Now, copy and paste the designs and update the text for all your recipes, as shown in the picture below. (Tip – You can use your keyboard shortcuts like "Ctrl + C" (to copy) and "Ctrl + V" (to paste) instead of selecting the image and clicking on "Edit" from the "Edit bar" to view the dropdown option for "Copy" and "Paste".)

Step 6

Click on "Save" at the top right corner of the screen and enter a name for your project, for example, "Recipe Stickers," then click "Save," as shown in the picture below.

Step 7

Your design is ready to be cut. Simply click on the "Make It" button on the top right corner of the screen. All the required mats and materials will be displayed on the screen. (Tip: You can move your design on the mat by simply dragging and dropping it anywhere on the mat to resemble the cutting space for your material on the actual cutting mat).

Step 8

Once you have loaded the sticker paper to your "Cricut" cutting machine, click "Continue" at the bottom right corner of the screen to start cutting your design.

Step 9

Once your "Cricut" device has been connected to your computer, set the cut setting to "Vinyl" (recommended to cut the sticker paper since it tends to be thicker than regular paper). Place the sticker paper on top of the cutting mat and load it into the "Cricut" device by pushing it against the rollers. The "Load/Unload" button would already be flashing, so just press that button first, followed by the flashing "Go" button. Viola! You have just created your very own recipe stickers.

Wedding Invitations

Materials needed – "Cricut" cutting machine, cutting mat, and cardstock or your choice of decorative paper/crepe paper/fabric, home printer (if not using "Cricut Maker").

Step 1

Use your "Cricut ID" to log in to the "Design Space" application. Then click on the "New Project" button on the top right corner of the screen to start a new project and view a blank canvas.

Step 2

A beginner-friendly way to create wedding invitations is a customization of an already existing project from the "Design Space" library that aligns with your own ideas. Click on the "Projects" icon on the "Design Panel" then select "Cards" from the "All Categories" drop-down.

Step 3

You can click on the project to preview its description and requirements. Once you have found the project you want to use, click "Customize" at the bottom of the screen, so you can edit the invite and add the required text to it.

Step 4

The design will be loaded on to the canvas. Click on the "Text" button and type in the details for your invite. You will be able to modify the font, color as well as alignment of the text from the "Edit Text Bar" on top of the screen. You can even adjust the size of the entire design as needed. (An invitation card can be anywhere from 6 to 9 inches wide)

Step 5

Select the entire design and click on the "Group" icon on the top right of the screen under "Layers Panel." Then click on the "Save" button to enter a name for your project and click "Save" again.

Step 6

Your design can now be printed then cut. Simply click on the "Make It" button on the top right corner of the screen to view the required mats and material. Then use your home printer to print the design on your chosen material (white cardstock or paper), or if using the "Cricut Maker," then just follow the prompts on the "Design Space" application.

Step 7

Load the material with printed design to your "Cricut" cutting machine and click "Continue" at the bottom right corner of the screen to start cutting your design.

Step 8

Once your "Cricut" device has been connected to your computer, set the cut setting to "cardstock." Then place the printed cardstock on top of the cutting mat and load it into the "Cricut" device by pushing against the rollers. The "Load/Unload" button would already be flashing, so just press that button first, followed by the flashing "Go" button. Viola! You have your wedding invitations all ready to be put in an envelope and on their way to all your wedding guests.

Custom Notebooks

Materials needed – "Cricut" cutting machine, cutting mat, and washi sheets or your choice of decorative paper/crepe paper/fabric.

Step 1

Use your "Cricut ID" to log in to the "Design Space" application. Then click on the "New Project" button on the top right corner of the screen to start a new project and view a blank canvas.

Step 2

Let's use an already existing project from the "Cricut" library for this. Click on the "Projects" icon on the "Design Panel" and type in "notebook" in the search bar. You can view all the projects available by clicking on them, and a pop-up window displaying all the details of the project will appear on your screen.

Step 3

Select the project that you like and click on "Customize," so you can further edit this project to your preference.

Step 4

The selected project will be displayed on the Canvas. You can check from the "Layers Panel" if your design contains only one layer, which is very easy to modify, or multiple layers that can be selectively modified. Click on the "Linetype Swatch" to view the color palette and select the desired color for your design.

Step 5

Once you have modified the design to your satisfaction, it is ready to be cut. Simply click on the "Make It" button on the top right corner of the screen to view the required mats and material for your project.

Step 6

Load the washi paper sheet to your "Cricut" cutting machine and click "Continue" at the bottom right corner of the screen to start cutting your design.

Step 7

Connect your "Cricut" device to your computer and place the washi paper or your chosen paper on top of the cutting mat and load it into the "Cricut" machine by pushing against the rollers. The "Load/Unload" button would already be flashing, so just press that button first, followed by the flashing "Go" button. Viola! Your kids can now enjoy their uniquely customized notebook.

Paper Flowers

Materials needed – "Cricut" cutting machine, cutting mat, cardstock, and adhesive.

Step 1

Use your "Cricut ID" to log in to the "Design Space" application. Then click on the "New Project" button on the top right corner of the screen to start a new project and view a blank canvas.

Step 2

Click on the "Images" icon on the "Design Panel" and type in "flower" in the search bar. Then select the image that you like and click on the "Insert Images" button at the bottom of the screen.

Step 3

The selected image will be displayed on the canvas and can be edited using applicable tools from the "Edit Image Bar." Then copy and paste the flower five times and make them a size smaller than the preceding flower to create a variable size for depth and texture for the design. Click on the "Linetype Swatch" to view the color palette and select the desired color for your design.

Step 5

Once you have modified the design to your satisfaction, it is ready to be cut. Simply click on the "Make It" button on the top right corner of the screen to view the required mats and material for your project.

Step 6

Load the cardstock to your "Cricut" cutting machine and click "Continue" at the bottom right corner of the screen to start cutting your design.

Step 7

Connect your "Cricut" device to your computer and place the cardstock or your chosen paper on top of the cutting mat and load it into the "Cricut" machine by pushing against the rollers. The "Load/Unload" button would already be flashing, so just press that button first, followed by the flashing "Go" button.

Step 8

Once the design has been cut, simply remove the cut flowers and bend them at the center. Then, using the adhesive, stack the flowers with the largest flower at the bottom.

CHAPTER 10: PROJECTS AND IDEAS WITH GLASS

Etched Monogrammed Glass

Glasses are one of the most-used things in your kitchen, and it's impossible to have too many of them. It's actually quite easy to customize them with etching, and it will look as if a professional did it. Simply use glass etching cream that you can find at any craft store! Be sure to read the instructions and warning labels carefully before you begin. The vinyl will act as a stencil, protecting the parts of the glass that you don't want to etch. Be sure to take your time to get the vinyl smooth against the glass, especially where there are small bits. You don't want any of the cream to get under the edge of the vinyl. You can use the Cricut Explore One, Cricut Explore Air 2, or Cricut Maker for this project.

Supplies Needed

- A glass of your choice — make sure that the spot you want to monogram is smooth
- Vinyl
- Cutting mat
- Weeding tool or pick
- Glass etching cream

Instructions

- Open Cricut Design Space and create a new project.
- Select the "Image" button in the Design Panel and search for "monogram."
- Choose your favorite monogram and click "Insert."
- Place your vinyl on the cutting mat.
- Send the design to your Cricut.
- Use a weeding tool or pick to remove the monogram, leaving the vinyl around it.
- Remove the vinyl from the mat.

- Carefully apply the vinyl around your glass, making it as smooth as possible, particularly around the monogram.
- If you have any letters with holes in your monogram, carefully reposition those cutouts in their proper place.
- Following the instructions on the etching cream, apply it to your monogram.
- Remove the cream and then the vinyl.
- Give your glass a good wash.
- Enjoy drinking out of your etched glass!

Live, Love, Laugh Glass Block

Glass blocks are an inexpensive yet surprisingly versatile craft material. You can find them at both craft and hardware stores. They typically have a hole with a lid so that you can fill the blocks with the items of your choice. This project uses tiny fairy lights for a glowing quote block, but you can fill it however you'd like. The frost spray paint adds a bit of elegance to the glass and diffuses the light for a softer glow, hiding the string of the fairy lights. Holographic vinyl will add to the magical look, but you can use whatever colors you'd like. This features a classic quote that's great to have around your house, but you can change it. You can use the Cricut Explore One, Cricut Explore Air 2, or Cricut Maker for this project.

Supplies Needed
- Glass block
- Frost spray paint
- Clear enamel spray
- Holographic vinyl
- Vinyl transfer tape
- Cutting mat
- Weeding tool or pick
- Fairy lights

Instructions

- Spray the entire glass block with frost spray paint and let it dry.
- Spray the glass block with a coat of clear enamel spray and let it dry.
- Open Cricut Design Space and create a new project.
- Select the "Text" button in the Design Panel.
- Type "Live Love Laugh" in the text box.
- Use the dropdown box to select your favorite font.
- Arrange the words to sit on top of each other.
- Place your vinyl on the cutting mat.
- Send the design to your Cricut.
- Use a weeding tool or pick to remove the excess vinyl from the design.
- Apply transfer tape to the design.
- Remove the paper backing and apply the words to the glass block.
- Smooth down the design and carefully remove the transfer tape.
- Place fairy lights in the opening of the block, leaving the battery pack on the outside.
- Enjoy your decorative quote!

Unicorn Wine Glass

Who doesn't love unicorns? Who doesn't love wine? Bring them together with these glittery wine glasses! The outdoor vinyl will hold up to use and washing, and the Mod Podge will keep the glitter in place for years to come. Customize it even more with your own quote. You could use a different magical creature as well—mermaids go great with glitter too! Customize this to suit your tastes or to create gifts for your friends and family. Consider using these for a party and letting the guests take them home as favors! You can use the Cricut Explore One, Cricut Explore Air 2, or Cricut Maker for this project.

Supplies Needed

- Stemless wine glasses
- Outdoor vinyl in the color of your choice
- Vinyl transfer tape

- Cutting mat
- Weeding tool or pick
- Extra fine glitter in the color of your choice
- Mod Podge

Instructions

1. Open Cricut Design Space and create a new project.
2. Select the "Text" button in the Design Panel.
3. Type "It's not drinking alone if my unicorn is here."
4. Using the dropdown box, select your favorite font.
5. Adjust the positioning of the letters, rotating some to give a whimsical look.
6. Select the "Image" button on the Design Panel and search for "unicorn."
7. Select your favorite unicorn and click "Insert," then arrange your design how you want it on the glass.
8. Place your vinyl on the cutting mat, making sure it is smooth and making full contact.
9. Send the design to your Cricut.
10. Use a weeding tool or pick to remove the excess vinyl from the design. Use the Cricut BrightPad to help if you have one.
11. Apply transfer tape to the design, pressing firmly and making sure there are no bubbles.
12. Remove the paper backing and apply the words to the glass where you'd like them. Leave at least a couple of inches at the bottom for the glitter.
13. Smooth down the design and carefully remove the transfer tape.
14. Coat the bottom of the glass in Mod Podge, wherever you would like glitter to be. Give the area a wavy edge.
15. Sprinkle glitter over the Mod Podge, working quickly before it dries.
16. Add another layer of Mod Podge and glitter, and set it aside to dry.
17. Cover the glitter in a thick coat of Mod Podge.
18. Allow the glass to cure for at least 48 hours.
19. Enjoy drinking from your unicorn wine glass!

CHAPTER 11: PROJECTS AND IDEAS WITH CLOTHING

Easy Lacey Dress

Lace dresses are adorable, but they can be hard to get ahold of and difficult to make. Fake it without anyone knowing better using your Cricut! The iron-on vinyl will look just like lace, and it will stand up to your child's activities much better than the real thing. Don't limit yourself to children's clothes; add some vinyl lace to your own as well! White vinyl will look like traditional lace the most, you can do this in any color that coordinates with the dress that you have. Use a Cricut EasyPress or iron to attach the vinyl to the fabric. You can use the Cricut Explore One, Cricut Explore Air 2, or Cricut Maker for this project.

Supplies Needed
- Dress of your choice
- White heat transfer vinyl
- Cricut EasyPress or iron
- Cutting mat
- Weeding tool or pick

Instructions
- Open Cricut Design Space and create a new project.
- Select the "Image" button in the lower left-hand corner and search "vintage lace border."
- Choose your favorite lace border and click "Insert."
- Place your vinyl on the cutting mat.
- Send the design to your Cricut.
- Use a weeding tool or pick to remove the excess vinyl from the design.
- Place the design along the hem of the dress with the plastic side up. Add lace wherever you like, such as along the collar or sleeves.

- Carefully iron on the design.
- After cooling, peel away the plastic by rolling it.
- Dress your child up in her adorable lacey dress!

Dinosaur T-Shirt

Everyone loves dinosaurs, and kids can't have enough t-shirts. Use iron-on vinyl to create the perfect shirt for your fossil-loving child! The small designs on the sleeves add a little extra, bringing it up a level from your standard graphic t-shirt. Just as with the rest of these projects, you can use the same idea with different designs. Customize a shirt for any of your child's interests. The Cricut EasyPress or iron will help you attach the vinyl designs to the t-shirt. You can use the Cricut Explore One, Cricut Explore Air 2, or Cricut Maker for this project.

Supplies Needed
- T-shirt of your choice
- Green heat transfer vinyl
- Cricut EasyPress or iron
- Cutting mat
- Weeding tool or pick

Instructions
- Open Cricut Design Space.
- Select the "Image" button in the lower left-hand corner and search "dinosaur."
- Choose your favorite dinosaur and click "Insert."
- Select "Image" again and search for "fossils."
- Choose your favorite fossil and click "Insert."
- Copy the fossil once so that you have two of them.
- Place your vinyl on the cutting mat.
- Send the design to your Cricut.

- Use a weeding tool or pick to remove the excess vinyl from the design.
- Place the dinosaur in the center of the t-shirt, and a fossil on each sleeve, with the plastic side up.
- Carefully iron on the design.
- After cooling, peel away the plastic by rolling it.
- Show off the cool dinosaur t-shirt!

Flower Garden Tote Bag

You can never have too many tote bags, whether you use them as reusable shopping bags, giant purses, or anything else. Create this cute flower garden bag to carry wherever you need to, and keep nature right by your side all day! Choose your favorite flowers, and the more variety you have, the more interesting the bag will be to look at. Canvas bags are a nice neutral base that will last you years, but you can use this idea with a different type of tote as well. The white vinyl gives a silhouette effect, but you can use a different color or even make each flower its own color. You'll need a Cricut EasyPress or iron for the heat transfer vinyl. You can use the Cricut Explore One, Cricut Explore Air 2, or Cricut Maker for this project.

Supplies Needed
- Canvas tote bag
- White heat transfer vinyl
- Cricut EasyPress or iron
- Cutting mat
- Weeding tool or pick

Instructions
- Open Cricut Design Space and create a new project.
- Select the "Image" button in the lower left-hand corner and search "flowers."
- Choose your favorite flower and click "Insert."

- Continue with a variety of flowers, lining them up together to form a straight edge at the bottom.
- Place your vinyl on the cutting mat.
- Send the design to your Cricut.
- Use a weeding tool or pick to remove the excess vinyl from the design.
- Place the design along the bottom of the tote bag with the plastic side up.
- Carefully iron on the design.
- After cooling, peel away the plastic by rolling it.
- Carry around your new garden tote bag!

CHAPTER 12: PROJECTS AND IDEAS WITH FABRIC

Tassels

Tassels have almost endless uses. These are incredibly easy to make and can be customized to fit whatever purpose you want. Add them to the edges of pillows or blankets, hang them from a string to make a banner, use one as a keychain or zipper pull, and a million other things! You can also try making these with leather or faux leather for a classier look. Tassels are cute on just about everything. For best results, use your Cricut Maker for this project.

Supplies Needed

- 12" x 18" fabric rectangles
- Fabric mat
- Glue gun

Instructions

1. Open Cricut Design Space and create a new project.
2. Select the "Image" button in the lower left-hand corner and search "tassel."
3. Select the image of a rectangle with lines on each side and click "Insert."
4. Place the fabric on the cutting mat.
5. Send the design to the Cricut.
6. Remove the fabric from the mat, saving the extra square.
7. Place the fabric face down and begin rolling tightly, starting on the uncut side. Untangle the fringe as needed.
8. Use some of the scrap fabric and a hot glue gun to secure the tassel at the top.
9. Decorate whatever you want with your new tassels!

Monogrammed Drawstring Bag

Drawstring bags are quick and easy to use. They're just as easy to make! This includes steps for sewing the pieces together, but you could even use fabric glue if you're not great with a needle and thread. You can keep these bags handy for every member of your family to grab and go as needed. You can tell them apart with the monograms, or use a different design on each one to customize them to a certain use or just decorate it. You can even use these as gift bags! This project uses heat transfer vinyl for the designs, so you'll need your Cricut EasyPress or iron. For best results, use your Cricut Maker for this project.

Supplies Needed
- Two matching rectangles of fabric
- Needle and thread
- Ribbon
- Heat transfer vinyl
- Cricut EasyPress or iron
- Cutting mat
- Weeding tool or pick

Instructions
1. Open Cricut Design Space and create a new project.
2. Select the "Image" button in the lower left-hand corner and search "monogram."
3. Select the monogram of your choice and click "Insert."
4. Place the iron-on material shiny liner side down on the cutting mat.
5. Send the design to the Cricut.
6. Use the weeding tool or pick to remove excess material.
7. Remove the monogram from the mat.
8. Center the monogram on your fabric, then move it a couple of inches down so that it won't be folded up when the ribbon is drawn.
9. Iron the design onto the fabric.

10. Place the two rectangles together, with the outer side of the fabric facing inward.
11. Sew around the edges, leaving a seam allowance. Leave the top open and stop a couple of inches down from the top.
12. Fold the top of the bag down until you reach your stitches.
13. Sew along the bottom of the folded edge, leaving the sides open.
14. Turn the bag right side out.
15. Thread the ribbon through the loop around the top of the bag.
16. Use your new drawstring bag to carry what you need!

Paw Print Socks

Socks are the ultimate cozy item. No warm pajamas are complete without a pair! Add a cute, hidden accent to the bottom of your or your child's socks with little paw prints. Show off your love for your pet or animals, in general, every time you cuddle up! You can do this with almost any small design or even use text to add a quote to the bottom of your feet. You can use any type of socks you find comfortable. For the easiest read, make sure the sock color and vinyl color contrast. Or make them in the same color for a hidden design! The shine of the vinyl will stand out from the cloth in certain lights.

Since this uses heat transfer vinyl, you'll need your Cricut EasyPress or iron. You can use the Cricut Explore One, Cricut Air 2, or Cricut Maker for this project.

Supplies Needed
- Socks
- Heat transfer vinyl
- Cutting mat
- Scrap cardboard
- Weeding tool or pick
- Cricut EasyPress or iron

Instructions
1. Open Cricut Design Space and create a new project.
2. Select the "Image" button in the lower left-hand corner and search "paw prints."
3. Select the paw prints of your choice and click "Insert."
4. Place the iron-on material on the mat.
5. Send the design to the Cricut.
6. Use the weeding tool or pick to remove excess material.
7. Remove the material from the mat.
8. Fit the scrap cardboard inside of the socks.
9. Place the iron-on material on the bottom of the socks.
10. Use the EasyPress to adhere it to the iron-on material.
11. After cooling, remove the cardboard from the socks.
12. Wear your cute paw print socks!

Night Sky Pillow

The night sky is a beautiful thing, and you will love having a piece of it on a cozy pillow. Customize this with the stars you love most, or add constellations, planets, galaxies, and more! Adults and children alike can enjoy these lovely pillows.

A sewing machine will make this project a breeze to put together, or you can use a needle and thread. If you're not great at sewing, use fabric glue to close the pillow. Choose a soft fabric that you love so that you can cuddle up with this pillow.

Supplies Needed
- Black, dark blue, or dark purple fabric
- Heat transfer vinyl in gold or silver
- Cutting mat
- Polyester batting
- Weeding tool or pick
- Cricut EasyPress

Instructions
1. Decide the shape you want for your pillow and cut two matching shapes out of the fabric.
2. Open Cricut Design Space and create a new project.
3. Select the "Image" button in the lower left-hand corner and search "stars."
4. Select the stars of your choice and click "Insert."
5. Place the iron-on material on the mat.
6. Send the design to the Cricut.
7. Use the weeding tool or pick to remove excess material.
8. Remove the material from the mat.
9. Place the iron-on material on the fabric.
10. Use the EasyPress to adhere it to the iron-on material.
11. Sew the two fabric pieces together, leaving allowance for a seam and a small space open.
12. Fill the pillow with polyester batting through the small open space.
13. Sew the pillow shut.
14. Cuddle up to your starry pillow!

CONCLUSION

Thank you for making it to the end. Cricut machines are used in many different projects. They are a great tool to have, but you need to know how to take care of them if you want them to last a long time. When using your Cricut machine, make sure that the blades and the cutting mat are kept clean. If they are dirty they can cause problems while cutting, because the blade will not be able to cut through the material correctly. The friction from your material against the dirty blades can cause them to create scratches on your material.

Generally, people use this machine for cutting out words and pictures from scrapbooks or creating stencils for their scrapbooking projects. This can be done with or without a computer. You just have to put your material on the mat and make sure that it is properly aligned, then you place it face down onto the Cricut machine, making sure that its corners fit into place correctly. Then once you press on "cut" button down, using your finger, you can push down any materials that may be sticking up so that they do not get stuck in the blades. The blades are used to cut through your material. The Mat is what you put on the cutting board that the Cricut machine works on. There may be different sizes of these mats. When you look at the product description, it will tell you what size it is. Some of these machines come with one, and some come with two. The size will vary depending on what model of Cricut machine that you have or are purchasing. So some of them come with one and some with two. But there is always a mat included when you purchase the product, so make sure that you do not purchase a device without a mat as well as an extra mat attached to it as well.

The blade is used to slice through your material and cut it into layers. The cutting board should be kept dry so that it does not soak up any moisture from your watery glaze work. These devices can cost anywhere from $50 dollars all the way up to $150 dollars.

Rentals are another option for getting these machines at a cheaper price. You will need to check out the company's review website and see what kinds of companies they have available. There are many different places to rent these machines, such as craft stores and online shops that offer them. Make sure that you know where your machine is shipped from before purchasing it, otherwise you will be paying too much money for it. Cricut Machines are one of the newest tools that everyone has been using lately. It was created by someone who had a special love for designing on paper and then making something out of it so that he could then make copies for his friends and family members. After creating three thousand kits that were all different shapes, sizes, glaze colors, and engravings on them, he decided to start making the Cricut machine.

There is a machine that your machine can be compared to called "Ace". This was made by another person who had a love for designing on paper and gluing something together to create something new. This person was only fourteen at the time. This machine is called "Ace". It has all of the same features as a Cricut machine, but there are some limitations to what it can do. One of these limitations is that it does not have a design base, so you have to purchase that also and then download your images from the computer onto the board. It also requires a computer with an attached printer in order for this machine to work properly. Cricut machines are meant for people who want to create something new or find something unique. If you do not know how to use one, there are many online tutorials that will help you learn how to use them correctly by using different patterns or designs. If someone wants to purchase this product, they should be aware of where they are purchasing it from. They should check out the company's review website so that they can see if their company has many unhappy customers or if they have few complaints about them. They need to see if the company gives good service or if they just take the customer's money and send faulty products back.

I hope you have learned something!

CRICUT EXPLORE AIR 2 FOR BEGINNERS

The definitive guide for beginners to learning

how to maximize your cricut machine

PAMELA CRAFT

INTRODUCTION

The Cricut Air 2 is a fantastic tool for crafters and designers alike. Using the Cricut Air 2, you can cut out nearly anything with the press of a button. The Cricut Explore Air 2 is a great machine for those who want to make their own paper crafts. It's a more expensive option, but it's great for people who want to buy materials and create their projects from scratch. The Cricut Explore Air 2 is a cutting machine that is designed specifically for cross-stitching. It comes with two spools of thread and two cording kits.

The Cricut Air 2 is a great cutter for those who are just getting started. It's easy to use and gives you more control over your projects than the original Air. The Cricut Explore Air 2 is a must-have for any crafter. It's one of the best cutting machines on the market and offers an amazing amount of control. The Cricut Explore Air 2 is a cutting machine that allows you to cut and design on the go. It's portable, lightweight, and doesn't require power. The Cricut Explore Air 2 is an amazing machine and makes cutting vinyl so much easier. The Cricut Explore Air 2 is a relatively new cutting machine, but it has already earned the praises of many customers. This is a Cricut cutting machine that's been updated with new features. It's the first Cricut to have Bluetooth connectivity, and if you have any other Cricut machines, you can use them as well.

What is the History of the Cricut Explore Air 2 Machine?
The Cricut Explore Air 2 was released to the public in June 2017. On October 15, 2018, the company released an added product called the "Cricut Create." The main differences between the Cricut Explore Air 2 and Cricut Create are that the new create model is portable and can connect to a computer wirelessly. The Cricut Explore Air 2 must be plugged into a power source. It also does not have Bluetooth capabilities. These changes were clearly made to bring more versatility to consumers who want to take their machine on-the-go, but are not ready for a wireless machine yet.

The additional product was dubbed "Create" because of its ability to personalize engraved items, such as phone cases and water bottles. However, it is important to note that you cannot use this model for intricate details or large projects like signs or shirts, which are better done with a wireless system like the Cricut Explore Air 2.

In addition, the Cricut Explore Air 2 is one of the most upgraded machines in the company's history. It comes with many new features that were not available on past models, including Bluetooth capabilities, a full touch screen menu and an updated operating system.

"The Cricut Explore Air 2 is a powerful and versatile craft cutter that makes projects of all sizes simple and fun." (http://cricut.com/products/cricut-explore-air2). The company states that the machine features quality performance and cutting precision. In addition, it includes Bluetooth capabilities to make "connecting your Cricut Explore Air 2 to compatible devices like mobile phones, tablets or other computers super easy."

The air 2 also comes with over 1,000 built-in images, including 90 built-in fonts. It also has easy tools for adding your own images for projects you create on the site or from other image sources. With this new model, you can easily create time-saving projects such signs and shirts for businesses or families. Owners of the Cricut Explore Air 2 have given it five out of five stars on Amazon as of October 2018, with 216 reviews. Customers claim that the price is reasonable compared to other craft machines such as the Monster Earth 4 and the Cricut Imagine. Plus, customers say that even though there are more options with new products like the Cricut Create, they believe that they will still value their investment in their air 2 machine by learning how to use it better and using it for simple projects, such as cards or paper crafting.

The Cricut Explore Air 2 also comes with an affordable price compared to other machines of similar quality and features. The machine comes in at $299, a low cost when factoring in its high-quality performance, features and portability.

It comes with basic cutting tools without any additional accessories for a low cost out of the box, so you can start creating your own cards or invitations right away at home or even in your office on work days. If you need anything extra, you can pick up a few accessories to further expand its functionality.

Once customers have started using the Cricut Explore Air 2, they have begun to see a large number of positive reviews on Amazon with 5 stars out of 5. Customers are impressed with the price and quality of this new craft machine and go on to say that it is easy to use and that the accessories are affordable as well. This means that while there is a great variety of items to print on, customers are finding it relatively easy to make things like cards and invitations so they can focus more on crafting rather than finding new ways to save money. So far, many users agree that it seems like an upgrade from past models in terms of performance and quality for the price point.

The Cricut Explore Air 2 comes in at around $300. With that price, you get a worldwide cutting machine with Bluetooth capabilities. It comes with over 1,000 built-in images and a variety of fonts that will work well with your projects. They have a variety of tools to make it easier for you to add your own images into a project if you want to use other images. For example, the machine holds up to 720 sheets of paper and has an additional 160 sheets that come with the machine if you need them or want them for other projects. Battery life is also great due to its rechargeable battery, which will last up to 45 minutes on one charge. This helps get users through multi-hour cutting sessions without having to stop frequently or drain their batteries. The Cricut Explore Air 2 is easy enough for everyone, from beginners just getting used to using a cutting machine all the way up to professionals who want all the features they can get for their money out of craft fabricators like this one.

CHAPTER 1: HOW TO USE THE CRICUT EXPLORE AIR 2

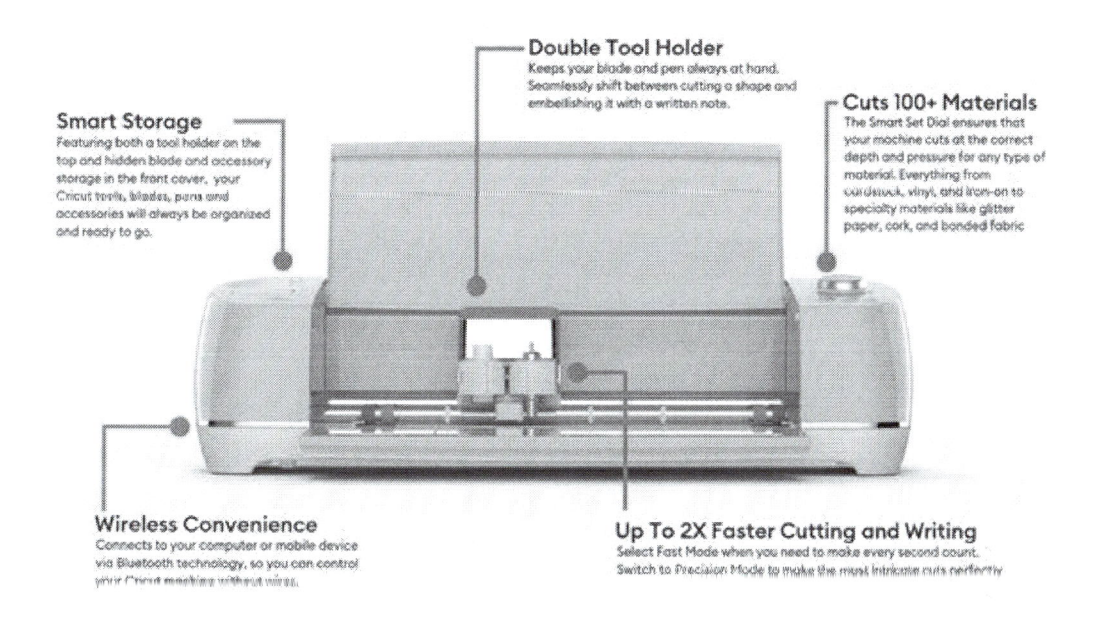

Smart Storage — Featuring both a tool holder on the top and hidden blade and accessory storage in the front cover, your Cricut tools, blades, pens and accessories will always be organized and ready to go.

Double Tool Holder — Keeps your blade and pen always at hand. Seamlessly shift between cutting a shape and embellishing it with a written note.

Cuts 100+ Materials — The Smart Set Dial ensures that your machine cuts at the correct depth and pressure for any type of material. Everything from cardstock, vinyl, and iron-on to specialty materials like glitter paper, cork, and bonded fabric.

Wireless Convenience — Connects to your computer or mobile device via Bluetooth technology, so you can control your Cricut machine without wires.

Up To 2X Faster Cutting and Writing — Select Fast Mode when you need to make every second count. Switch to Precision Mode to make the most intricate cuts perfectly.

The Cricut Explore Air 2 allows you to cut more than 100 types of materials from cardboard to vinyl, but it has a cutting force of 400gr, a much lower figure than that of the Maker. It lets you cut materials up to 2.4mm thick thanks to its 4kg cutting force. What does this mean? That the Cricut Maker allows you to cut many more materials such as balsa wood, chipboard, leather, etc. It has a special blade to cut thicker materials, the Knife Blade. Thanks to its gear system, it allows greater control of cutting tools, being able to cut materials with greater precision and force.

The Explore Air 2 has a dial on the machine itself where you can select the material you are going to cut, or you can put it in «Custom» to choose the material from Design Space. Instead, in Maker you choose it directly from the application.

Setting Up the Cricut Explore Air 2

Cricut Explore Air 2 combines the speed of a heat press with the comfort of iron, so you'll get consistent ironing results quickly and easily, even after repeated washes. Cricut Explore Air 2 was released in August 2017, and a 9 "x9" (25cm x 25cm) hot plate was issued in Sky color.

In 2018, Cricut Explore Air 2 joins Cricut Explore Air 2. A family of products in three sizes to fit a variety of 6"x7", 9"x9", 12"x10" iron projects. (Cricut Explore Air 2 sold separately). Cricut Explore Air 2 heats (higher temperature) and heats faster than the original model.

What's in the Box

- Explorer Air Cricut
- Security base
- Welcome book
- Practice project materials (for Cricut Explore Air 2, this includes a cotton storage bag).
- Warranty

Major Features

1. Easy to learn and use.
2. No press fabric is required for most substrates.
3. The original Cricut Explore Air 2 can be heated to 180°C (360°F).
4. Reliable heat up to 400°F (205°C) for Cricut Explore Air 2.
5. After repeated washings, complex transfer deposits
6. Great for large or layered iron projects.
7. Lightweight, portable, and easy to store.
8. Compatible with almost every major brand of heat transfer material.

Even though Cricut Explore Air 2 can be used wirelessly/Bluetooth, let's start by setting it up with the USB cable. Begin by setting it on a surface with at least 10 " free at the back, as the cutting base will move back and forth inside the machine. Finishing the machine setup, it will automatically register the machine to your account. To set up your Cricut Explore Air 2 and any other Cricut machine series follow these steps below:

1. MAC/IPAD/PC
2. Connect the machine by connecting the power adapter and the USB cable.
3. Turn on your Explore Air 2 machine and also your computer.
4. Visit the Cricut website, register, and download the latest plugin software for a user account.
5. Head on to design.cricut.com and run the installer.
6. Click the menu icon in the upper left-hand corner and choose New Machine Settings.
7. ANDROID AND IOS
8. Connect the machine and turn it on.
9. Pair your Android or iOS device with the Cricut machine via Bluetooth.
10. Go ahead to download and install the Design Space app.
11. Launch the application, then log in or create a Cricut ID.
12. Touch the menu and select Machine configuration.

13. Select your machine model and follow the on-screen instructions to complete the setup.
14. You will be guided through the installation process and your first project, a thank you card.

Why Choose Cricut Explore Air 2

Cricut Explore Air 2 delivers professional ironing results within 60 seconds. Combining the speed of a heat press with the convenience of a home iron, the Cricut Explore Air 2 is free from guesswork and gives you fast, smooth results with a good wash after washing. Use the handy interactive quick reference guide to determine the correct time and temperature settings for your project, apply the press to your design with gentle pressure, and beep when you hear it! With adjustable heat settings, Cricut Explore Air 2 works beautifully not only on aluminum, glass, and metal projects but also on large layered projects. Convenient security features include a private security dock and automatic shutdown. Cricut Explore Air 2 is lightweight, comfortable to carry, easy to store, and compatible with all major brands of heat transfer materials. And of course, it's perfect for all Cricut cutting machines.

What Do You Need to Succeed?

Three conditions must be met that work together to achieve professional results at home.
- Uniform Heat
- Exact temperature
- Plane

Controls

Cricut Explore Air 2's simple controls are the key to iron's success. You will love the results.

Tip

- See the interactive quick reference guide to find the correct time and temperature settings for your specific ironing project.
- Always use Cricut Explore Air 2 at room temperature.
- Before using Cricut Explore Air 2, make sure the fabric and other base materials are completely dry.
- Always return Cricut Explore Air 2 to its safety base when not in use.
- Before using Cricut Explore Air 2, make sure there is no tape or protective film on the control panel.

Let's Start

- Power on Cricut Explorer Air 2 by pressing the power button on the left side of the screen.
- Find a firm, flat, heat-resistant surface around your waist.
- Avoid a thin iron board.

Set the exact ratio of timer and temperature.

- Press the timer button and then use the +/- buttons to select the time to heat the ironing project.
- Click the temperature button and then use the +/- buttons to select the desired temperature. The Cricut Explore Air 2 will begin to heat up, and the display will show the temperature going up or down. The Cricut button turns orange while adjusting the temperature and turns green when the desired temperature is reached. Cricut Explore Air 2 beeps when ready to use.

Note: Cricut Explore Air 2 operates at high temperatures and can cause burns and other injuries. Use with extreme caution.

- Preheat the substrate.

- Place Cricut Explore Air 2 on the fabric for 3-5 seconds to remove wrinkles and moisture.
- Place the design.
- Place the map where you want it.
- Make sure the shiny side (clear coating) is facing up.
- Heat both sides.
- Place Cricut Explore Air 2 in your design and press the Cricut button to start the timer.
- Hold Cricut Explore Air 2 in place and press gently until you hear a beep.
- Turn the substrate over and heat the back of the design for 10-15 seconds.
- Before removing the liner, refer to the Interactive Quick Reference Guide to determine if the coating needs to be stripped while it is hot or if it should be allowed to cool completely.

Cricut Explore Air 2: Recommended Configuration

The list of recommended Cricut Explore Air 2 configurations will be updated as additional base materials are tested and other ferrous products are released.

- View Cricut Explore Air 2 Interactive Quick Reference Guide
- Download printable PDF

How Do You Use Layer Technology?

Create a masterpiece of multi-colored textures using an iron technique called "layers."

How Do You Overlay Your Iron Designs?

- Almost every Cricut images are designed with multiple layers that come together to form a composite image. Design the image on the Cricut machine and cut it into segments. Before cutting, mirror your design in Design Space to ensure that the image layers are correctly oriented when applied to the base material.

- Plugin and power on Cricut Explore Air 2.
- Set the Cricut Explore Air 2 temperature and timer to the recommended settings for the base material. Find the right settings with this interactive quick reference guide.
- Preheat the base metal in Cricut Explore Air 2 for the time recommended in the bill of material.
- Place the bottom layer of the image on top of the base material, cover with Cricut Explore Air 2 and press firmly for 1-3 seconds.
- Hard pressure means using both hands and considerable weight. A waist-high table will help you apply firm pressure.
- Put Cricut Explore Air 2 back on the safety base and immediately remove the coating from the applied image layer. This is called a "hot shell."
- The adhesive does not "cure" at this time, but using heat with each additional coat will adequately cure the resin on all layers.
- Repeat steps 5 and 6.
- Before applying heat to each new layer, make sure that the exposed iron film on each previous coat is completely covered and protected by the liner. "Exposed film" refers to areas of iron that are not covered by a new layer of metal.
- Topcoat: When adding a coat to your image, use Easy Press for 15 seconds to apply firm pressure.
- Turn the substrate over and apply heat and pressure firmly from the back for 10-15 seconds.

What Kind of Iron Can Be Used When Stacking?

Every Cricut Iron-On product can be used in projects.

- Sparkle foil, glitter, and holographic plates are only recommended as topcoats.
- Unnecessary textures may appear when repeatedly applying heat on the Foil Iron-On.

- Do not stack glitter iron-on films. Due to its luster, all ferrous materials applied to glitter iron-on film do not adhere well and can come off.

Realizing Your First Project

Cutting Letters and Shapes for Scrapbooking

Shapes are one of the most vital features in Cricut Design Space. They are used for creating some of the best designs. In this tutorial, you will learn how to cut letters or texts, how to add shapes and how to adjust the size, colors and rotate shapes.

To add a shape;

- Log into your Design Space.
- From the drop-down menu, click "Canvas". You will be taken to the canvas or work area.
- Click "Shapes" on the left panel of the canvas.
- A window will pop-up with all the shapes available in Cricut Design Space.
- Click to add shape.
- We have explained the process of adding a shape. To cut a shape;
- Click "Linetype". Linetype lets your machine know whether you plan on cutting, drawing or scoring a shape.
- Select "Cut" as Linetype and proceed with cutting the shape.

Cutting Letters

Cutting letters or texts is simple if you know how to do it. To cut letters;

- First of all, you need to add the text you want to cut. Click "Add Text" on the left panel of the canvas.
- Place text in the area where you want to cut it. Highlight text and click on the slice tool. If you have multiple lines of texts, weld them and create a single layer. Then use the slice tool.
- Move the sliced letters from the circle and delete the ones you don't need.

CHAPTER 2: WHAT IT CAN CUT WITH CRICUT EXPLORE AIR 2

In this, you will find some information about what materials the Cricut Explore Air 2 can cut. This is a list of materials that we have used and have been able to cut successfully on our Cricut Explore Air 2 machine. It is important to note that each material will need different blade settings for the best results when using this machine. Some materials might even require a few tries to get right, depending on your settings. We recommend going through many test cuts before starting on your final product to ensure your settings are correct.

Materials that can be cut successfully:

Cardboard, craft paper, wood, vinyl, fabric.
*Some materials will need to be cut thin.
Materials that we have NOT been able to cut successfully**:
Plastic (Brocade, Vinyl, etc.), wire, leather, masonite, vinyl or fabric *plastic and metal are not recommended for the Cricut Explore air 2 unless you are cutting smaller pieces. We recommend using Steel blades for most plastics and metals.
Materials that we recommend trying before getting a feel for the machine:
Vinyl is most likely not going to cut well on the Cricut Explore Air 2 due to the thickness of the material that is comparable with laser cutting boards of other machines. You might be able to experiment with it in case you put your blade too close together or at an angle at certain points, but for safety reasons we do not recommend this method. Although we haven't tried it yet, any thick material like Masonite is very likely not going to work on the Explore Air 2 as well because of how hard it is and how thick it can get. We recommend doing test cuts on thin sheets of Masonite or using the same method as we have with the vinyl to experiment.

*Bad materials will not cut correctly on your machine. Thin materials are recommended, and you should use medium to thick gauge when cutting for best results.

**The Cricut Explore Air 2 can only cut thin sheet metal or plastic, anything above 1/4" is not recommended. Thick materials like wood won't even be visible on some images because they are too thick for this machine. **The Cricut Explore Air 2 cannot cut cards other than ones similar to a postcard. We recommend trying out scraps of different thickness cardstock before attempting anything larger than a postcard size.

Ways to get the most out of your Cricut Explore Air 2 cutter:

The Cricut Explore Air 2 was designed to cut on and through solid materials. The best way to use this machine is with a laser cutting or cutting mat such as the one we have for sale on our store's website. The Explore Air 2's jaws are so small it can fit in between intricate patterns and cuts very accurately. When you are cutting into wood, make sure you take extra care that you do not leave splinters behind. This can cause your machine to jam.

If you are using a wooden surface and need coarse settings, something like 1/8" or 1/4" will work well for most materials, and we recommend starting at that size when starting on your project. For some thicker board materials, we recommend using a medium to thick gauge depending on your choice of paper or vinyl.

Be very careful if you are cutting into cardstock or other materials that are not paper-based. These materials can jam your machine, and you will need to unjam the machine from the inside of the lid. If your material is getting clogged, there is something wrong with your settings, or you are struggling with something more difficult, do not give up. Try a different blade for different results and remember that this machine was built by an actual company worker for people who love to craft and like to change things up.

We recommend having a good understanding of what you are doing before using this brand new machine on anything more than paper or light fabrics and cardboard in case it jams. If you aren't sure what settings to use, we recommend coming back another day when you have done a few test prints first to get a feel for how the Explore 2 works for you. As always, our support team is here to help if you can't figure it out on your own.

**The Explore Air 2 and the Explore Air were both sold as separate machines. They work the same way and can cut the same materials. **The Cricut Explore Air 2 can now be purchased as a twin to the Cricut Maker machine. This means that it comes with a set of blades similar to what you would get when purchasing a Cricut Maker bundle, which includes wood, metal, and plastic blades along with a clear, textured, and black matte blade for exact cuts.

CHAPTER 3: DIFFERENCES BETWEEN CRICUT MAKER AND CRICUT EXPLORE AIR 2

Model Overview: Maker vs. Air 2

When Cricut Maker was unveiled to the public in the summer of 2017, one of the more interesting questions was; how does it compare to Cricut Explore Air 2?

It's a valid question because Cricut Explore 2 (a fantastic machine) had just been released and is by all standards a fantastic cutting machine. The truth is that both are excellent self-contained machines that are extremely efficient for what they were designed for, however, there are pros and cons associated with both, and any craftsman will be better suited to either. The meeting between Cricut Maker and Explore Air 2 has begun, and this is an opportunity for you to take a closer look at the right choice for you.

Here are some comparisons:

Versatility

In terms of versatility, there is only one winner: The Cricut Maker!
The Cricut machine does 100% of what the Explore Air 2 can do and more. It consists of a system of adaptive tools capable of cutting over 100 different materials and an extensive library of sewing patterns. When you consider all of this, you will realize that Cricut Maker is versatile enough to work with a variety of tools, including all kinds of blades released by Circuit, brand new knives and spinning blades, and yet to release those too.

Look no further because the rotating blade that comes with Cricut Maker during purchase already places it on top of the Explore Air 2. The blade does not need support or support material because it easily cuts all types of fabric.

In theory, the Explore Air 2 is capable of cutting fabric, but it's not as good as the Maker. Therefore, a support material is always needed because the thin blade often catches on the fabric. Also, users of the Explore Air 2 machine always use separate fabric cutters to get the cuts they want, but conversely, the Maker is an all-purpose machine that does it all.

Cutting Specifications

When we talk about cutting specifications, we mean the machine that cuts best. Plus, the cut is why people even go out to buy the car in the first place. If you consider the price (base price) of the Cricut Explore Air 2, you will agree with me that it is extremely affordable. The machine remains one of the best cutters around because its German-made carbide blade cuts through materials with extreme ease, which is why it is used to make small and intricate designs. In contrast, Cricut Maker features blades that are not only sharp and precise, but also possess a lot more strength behind them; Cricut Maker has around 4,000 grams of strength, while the Explore Air comes with just 400 grams.

Cricut Maker cuts easier and tidier, requires fewer passes on thicker materials, and can work with far more materials than Explore Air. Additionally, the Marker is designed to potentially work with newer and more sophisticated blades (such as the knife blade and the rotary blade), as opposed to the Explore Air. In terms of fabric cutting, the rotary blade remains a revolutionary invention that has greatly improved the industry, however, the knife blade has proven to be safer and more effective; it is the ultimate tool for cutting thick materials.

Explore Air 2 is a highly efficient cutting machine that is perfectly suited for craftsmen who stick to thin materials and require no special intervention. The maximum cut size of both machines is 12 "wide by 24" long, and most industry experts think that the Maker's cut size should have been increased to at least the size of the Silhouette Cameo 3 (12 "wide by 10" long).

Price

Cricut Maker is an improved version of the Explore Air 2; however, many people believe that those improved features cannot justify the price increase. Cricut Maker is listed for $399.99 on the Cricut website, and while it comes with improved features, many people see it as a significant amount to put on a cutter. On the other hand, the Explore Air 2 is priced at $299.99, and during sales, the price drops significantly.

Longevity

In general, when people evaluate options for the products they intend to buy, most of the time they consider price before other factors, but the truth is, price isn't everything. So, another factor to watch out for is the longevity of the products. In terms of longevity, the Cricut Maker and Explore Air 2 are very solid machines, and there is no question of their durability.

However, the Maker appears to be better suited for the future because the cutter will eventually outlive that of the Explore Air 2. Additionally, Cricut Maker comes with the Adaptive Tool System, which means it is guaranteed to be compatible with all types of blades and tools that will be released shortly. No matter how much the creative process evolves over the next couple of years, Cricut Maker will remain effective and relevant.

On the other hand, the Explore Air 2 isn't designed to deliver more than it already does, and while it won't become obsolete, it simply can't support the new blades and tools that are released by Cricut. By comparison, the Explore Air 2 is meant for people who are happy with the options available and concerned about improving their skills, while Cricut Maker is suitable for people who intend to experiment and further develop their crafts.

Software

In terms of software, there is nothing that separates these two machines because they both use Cricut Design Space software. Design Space Software is a decent program that is easy to use and contains many editing options to allow users to effectively customize their designs. Additionally, there is a store that contains hundreds of editing options that users can use and customize their designs. Users can upload their designs and convert them for free, so advanced users can create their complex designs in more sophisticated programs like Adobe Illustrator, Corel Draw, Make the Cut, and Sure Cuts a Lot.

Cricut Design Space is cloud-based, so users can design on their personal computers, tablets and phones. It's an easy program to use, but it has its flaws: it gets flawed and limiting at times, especially when creating new designs within the program.

Sewing projects

In terms of use for sewing projects, it's not a contest! Explore Air 2 is a versatile machine, but it falls short of Cricut Maker. On the other hand, aside from the current sewing machine, Cricut Maker is what people use for serious sewing projects. The Maker comes with a library that contains many sewing patterns and will not only cut the sewing patterns; He also marks them with the washable fabric marker. The Cricut Maker takes the guesswork out of marking templates, and this ultimately improves the final output of the job.

Portability

One of the most important but often overlooked features of machines is portability. If you are a craftsman who prefers to be static, then you can overlook it, but if you are someone who prefers to travel with your cutting machine, then you need to consider the size of the machine. Of the two machines, the Cricut Maker is the heaviest, weighing nearly 24 pounds, versus the Explore Air 2, which weighs just 14.8 pounds.

Cricut Maker is a static machine designed specifically for use in a specialized space, home or craft room. It has plenty of storage space and even comes with a provision for charging phones and/or tablets. Explore Air 2 is agile and comes with a smaller amount of storage, so it's perfect for people who like to work on the road. In terms of portability and ease of movement, the Explore Air 2 is higher than the Cricut Maker.

Easy to Use

Both machines are relatively easy to use with little practice, but in terms of ease of use, Cricut Maker sits alongside the Explore Air 2. Explore Air 2 is built with the Smart Set Dial on the front, and this allows users to easily select from the most common materials. Once the knob is set, the machine automatically adjusts the cutting settings accordingly. However, the problem most users face is that most of the materials used by most cutters aren't always the most common materials for members of the wider Cricut community. Therefore, you need to manually set the material settings from Design Space if the material is not on the dial.

It's not an extremely difficult process, but it's a little frustrating, especially when you have to go through the same procedure over and over again. On the other hand, Cricut Maker automatically adjusts its settings based on the type of material loaded on the cutting mat. It is extremely simple, and the user does not need to make any settings.

Cartridges

Newcomers to the world of Cricut and craft cutting may not understand this, however, longtime Cricut users will know all about cartridges - they may even have a space dedicated to them in their craft rooms. It is no longer mandatory to use cartridges for projects on both Cricut Maker and Explore Air 2. However, in case you have a couple of old cartridges at home, you may want to use them; then you can directly connect them to Explore Air 2 and use them.

You can use cartridges with Cricut Maker, but it's a little more complex. You will need to get hold of the cartridge adapter, which will allow you to connect the physical cartridges to the Design Space. The Cartridge Adapter Connection uses a USB port to connect cartridges with the Maker. There is also the option of using digital cartridges instead of purchasing the adapter. Digital cartridges are downloaded directly into Design Space.

Print and Then Cut
The last and final battle between the Explorer Air 2 and Cricut Maker is which of the machines has a better one for Print Then Cut. Cricut Maker comes with the Print Then Cut (PtC) feature, which allows users to print their designs onto white paper and then cut. This feature is useful for crafters who tend to experiment more on new designs instead of simply downloading designs from Cricut Design Space.

The Explore Air 2 also has the same PtC function as the Cricut Maker, however, the difference is that the Cricut Maker can PtC on colored and patterned paper, while the Explore Air 2 cannot. Therefore, in terms of Print Then Cut, Cricut Maker stands alongside Explore air 2.

General Verdict
At this point, Circuit Maker is the best machine. It is more durable, offers better print and cut functionality, easier to use, more versatile, and a better all-around cutter. The Explore Air 2 is a very good machine that has been serving artisans for some time and will continue to do so in the future; however, Cricut Maker is just too good for that.

Explore Air is the perfect machine for artisans who use paper, thin materials, cartridges and even those on a tight budget. Both machines are highly efficient and serve their purposes perfectly; Cricut Maker is for makers, while Explore Air 2 is for artisans cutting.

CHAPTER 4: CHOOSE THE BEST ACCESSORIES FOR CRICUT EXPLORE AIR 2

Cricut Tools and Accessory

Cricut Explore Cutting Blades

Both Cricut Explore Machines come with an extremely sharp German carbide fine-point blade. This allows all users to get started cutting right away. It comes already housed within the Cricut machine and is easily removable and sharpened in the event that the blade gets dull. A user tip on keeping your blade sharp and long-lasting is to stick the blade into a ball... This allows you to continue using the same blade for an extended period of time and saving you money as well! A fine- point cutting blade is typically used for almost all of the Cricut design cutting projects and will last through many projects when taken care of properly. If you are continually cutting rough materials, it is recommended to sharpen the blade often. The housing for this blade is silver on the older style machines and has been upgraded to gold for the new generation of machines.

The following type of blade that is commonly used is the Deep Cut Blade. This is the type of blade you will need in order to cut thicker materials. These materials include thin wood and leather. You heard that right; you can cut leather with a Cricut machine! With this blade, you will need to get its custom housing piece, which you can purchase separately. When using this blade, you will simply need to swap out the housing pieces and then attach the blade as necessary. Similarly, as the fine-point blade, you will need to take care of this blade and sharpen it often. Since you are using thick materials for this blade, you may have to replace it more often if using it all the time. The housing for this type of cut blade is black. You also will have the option to purchase cut blades individually once you have the housing unit.

Cutting Mats

Cricut cutting mats come in a variety of sizes and degree of stickiness. Depending on what material you are using, you will want less or more stickiness on your mat. Standard grip Mats can be used for most of your project cutting needs. You are able to cut cardstock, vinyl, and iron-on, etc., with this mat. There is also a Pink Fabric cutting mat, something that is necessary when cutting any time of fabric with a Cricut machine. It comes in a 12"x12" size or a 12"x24" size, depending on how large your project cut is.

The Circuit Weeder

The weeder tool, which looks similar to a dental pick, is used for removing negative space from a vinyl project. This weeder tool is a must when doing any type of project that involves vinyl. Trying to get rid of access vinyl is nearly impossible without a weeder, especially with materials like glitter iron-on. A weeder is a useful tool for any type of project using adhesives. Instead of picking up the adhesive with your fingertips, use the weeder tool and keep your fingers free of a sticky mess!

The Cricut Scraper

The Circuit Scraper tool is essential (and a lifesaver!) when you need to rid your cutting mat of excess negative bits. This tool typically works best with paper, such as cardstock, but other materials can easily be scraped up as well. Use the flexibility of the mat to your advantage as you scrap the bits off the mat to ensure you are not scraping up the adhesive on the mat as well. You can also use the Cricut Scraper as a score line holder, which allows you to fold over the scoreline with a nice crisp edge. It can also be used as a burnishing tool for Cricut transfer tape, as it will allow seamless separation of the transfer tape from the backing.

The Cricut Spatula

A spatula is a must-have tool for a crafter who works with a lot of paper. Pulling the paper off of a Cricut cut mat can result in a lot of tearing and paper curling if you are not diligent and mindful when you are removing it. The spatula is thinly designed to slip right under paper, which allows you to ease it off the mat carefully. Be sure to clean it often, as adhesive is likely to build up after several uses.

The Cricut Tweezers

Projects that involve a lot of embellishments will require a pair of tweezers. The Cricut tweezers can be a bit awkward to use at first, as they function directly opposite than we are used to with traditional tweezers. They need to be squeezed to open them, as opposed to squeezing them to shut. Ultimately you will begin to realize the genius behind this design because you will be able to pick something up and release pressure on it as the Cricut tweezers will hold pressure on the object. You'll save yourself from continuously dropping small pieces and many hand cramps!

The Cricut Scissors

Using the right scissors for a job can make a world of difference. The Cricut Scissors are made from stainless steel to ensure they will stick around for many jobs before getting dull. The scissors come with a micro-tip blade, so finer details in smaller areas are easier and clean right down to a point.

The Cricut Scoring Tool

If you want to do projects that involve a scoring line, such as folding cards in half or making 3D boxes, you will want to invest in a Cricut Scoring tool. You can insert this tool into the second tool holder, or accessory clamp, into the Cricut Explore itself, and the Cricut will use it to make score lines wherever the design dictates. They will need to be present in the Cricut Design Space file in order for the machine to recognize the scoreline is needed in the project.

The basic tool kit sold by Cricut does not come with a scoring tool, you will need to purchase this separately. If you plan to work with a lot of paper projects, this is a worthy tool to invest in.

The Cricut Easy Press
If you begin to venture into iron-on projects and want to upgrade from a traditional iron and ironing board, the Cricut Easypress is the right way to go. It will make projects so much easier than using a traditional iron. The Cricut Easypress is known to help keep designed adhered for longer, essentially no more peeling of designs after one or two uses and washes. The Easypress also takes all of the guesswork out of the right amount of contact time as well as temperature. You will not run the peril of burning your transfer paper or fabric!

The Cricut Brightpad
Brightpad reduces eyestrain while making crafting easier. It is designed to illuminate fine lines for tracing, cut lines for weeding, and so much more! It is thin and lightweight, which allows for durable transportation. The only downfall to this accessory is that it must be plugged in while it is used. It does not contain a rechargeable battery.

The Cricut Cuttlebug Machine
The Cricut Cuttlebug is an embossing and dies cutting machine that offers portability and versatility when it comes to cutting and embossing. This machine gives professional-looking results with clean, crisp, and deep embosses. This machine goes beyond paper, allowing you to emboss tissue paper, foils, thin leather, and more! We sincerely hope this unit gives you a better understanding of the tools and accessories that can be used with the Cricut cutting machines and how best to put them into use when designing and creating your own projects! Know that these tools are here to make your life easier it's worth investing in them!

Cricut Mats

Cricut cutting mat is where the cutting takes place. You have to clean and maintain your Cricut cutting mat. If the cutting mat isn't clean, it can stain the machine. Also, if your cutting mat has stopped sticking, it can spoil your designs and creations.

When your mat is no longer sticky because of debris and grime, cleaning it and making it sticky again will bring it back to life. The solutions that I will mention are not ideal for the pink cutting mats, only for the green, blue, and purple.

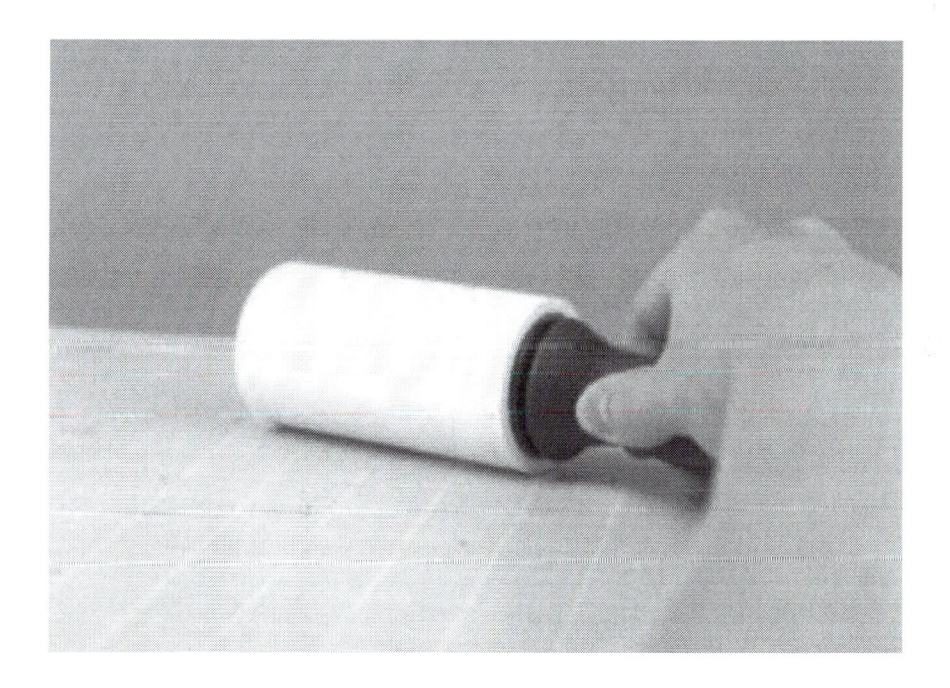

There are many ways to clean your cutting mat.

- Using baby wipes:

Make use of alcohol-free, unscented, and bleach-free baby wipes to clean your mat. You should use the plainest baby wipes that you can find so that you don't add lotions, cornstarch, solvents or oils to your cutting mat. If not, you could affect the stickiness and adhesive of the mat. Also, after cleaning it, let it dry completely before using it.

- Using a Sticky Lint Roller

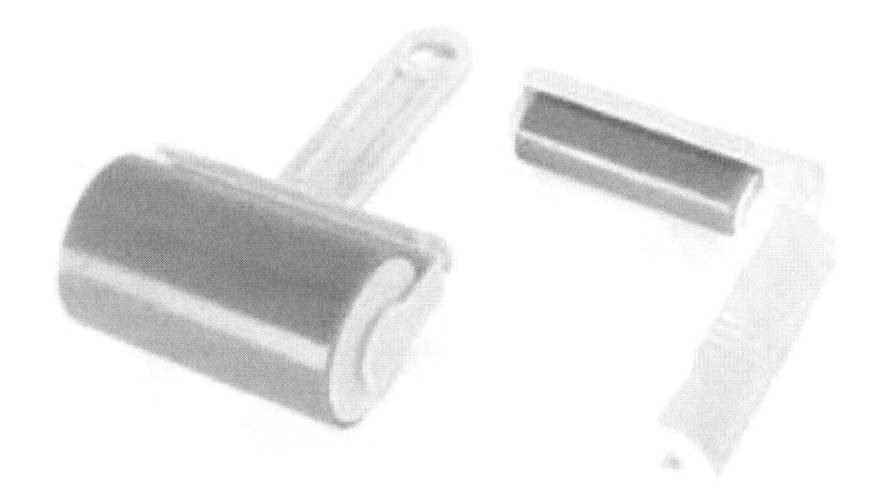

You can also use a roll of masking tape if you don't find a sticky lint roller. Run the roll across the mat to get rid of hairs, fibers, specks of dust, and paper particles. This form of cleaning can be done daily or between projects so that dust doesn't accumulate on the mat. This is a fast way to remove dirt apart from using tweezers or scrapers.

- Using warm water with soap

You can also clean the mat with soap and warm water. You should also use the plainest soap possible so that you don't mess with the mat. Use a clean cloth, sponge, soft brush, or a magic eraser. Also, rinse it thoroughly and don't use it until it is completely dry.

- Using an adhesive remover

In the case of heavy-duty cleaning, then you should use a reliable adhesive remover to clean it properly. When using an adhesive remover, read the directions properly before you start. Then, spray a little amount on the mat and spread it around with a scraper or anything that can act as a makeshift scraper.

After this, wash the mat with warm water and soap in case there is leftover residue and let it dry properly.

How to Make Your Cutting Mat Sticky Again

After washing or cleaning your cutting mat, you have to make them sticky again. The most advisable way to make your mat sticky again is by adding glue to it. Get a solid glue stick like the Zig 2-Way Glue Pen and apply it to the inner portion of the mat.

Then, stroke the glue around the mat and ensure that there is no glue residue on the edges of the mat. After about 30 minutes, the glue will turn clear. If the cutting mat turns out to be too sticky after you apply glue, you can use a piece of fabric to reduce the adhesive by pressing the material on the parts of the mat that are very sticky. Cover the mat with a clear film cover after a few hours. You can also use tacky glues or spray adhesives that are ideal for cutting mats.

General Maintenance

When your mat isn't in use, cover it with a clear film cover so that dust and hairs won't accumulate on the surface of the mat.

Handle your mats with care. If you want to ensure that the adhesive does not get damaged, avoid touching the sticky surface with your hands. Always ensure that your mat dries entirely before using it or covering it up. Don't use heat when drying your mat, but you can place it in front of a fan. Also, ensure that it is drying hanging up so that both sides will dry.

CHAPTER 5: CRAFT IDEAS FOR YOUR CRICUT CUTTING MACHINE

DIYs with Cricut Machine

It is too much fun to make designs with Cricut. Through your Cricut Explore cutting machines, you can make all types of crafts. There are so many excellent designs of Cricut to consider. You can find a large number of tutorials for tasks here.

Infusible Ink T-Shirt

Sanitize your hands with soap before you are starting this project and dry them fully. Cricut Infusible Ink can be extremely susceptible to heat and moisture. Remove the moisture or lotion on your hands. Try wearing any plastic gloves if your palms sweat constantly.

Supplies:

1. Standard Grip Mat
2. Cricut EasyPress Mat
3. Cricut t-shirt blank
4. Infusible Ink Transfer Sheet
5. White cardstock (80 lb)
6. Scissors
7. Cricut Maker or Cricut Explore cutting machine
8. Cricut EasyPress 2 or Cricut EasyPress
9. Sheets of butcher paper
10. Lint roller

Directions:

1. Step 1. On a green Regular Grip sheet with the color liner side down and color side up, put an Infusible Ink Transfer Mat.
2. Step 2. To get the free cut file you have created, head over to Design space. With a mermaid costume, ideal for summer and relaxing beach days, it says, "See you later." If required, resize the template, then follow the instructions to cut. Be sure the template is mirrored! Choose "Browse All Materials," then "Infusible Ink Transfer Sheet." Change the key to "Custom" first when working with the Cricut Explore machine. Load the blade and mat into the machine, then click the Go" lighting button to cut.
3. Step 3. Remove from the sheet the trimmed Infusible Ink Transfer board. For another task, use scissors to cut through the cut layout and keep the remaining transfer sheet. When treating Infusible Ink Transfer Sheets, make sure that there is no oil or sweat on your palms, leading to trouble while using the ink. Roll the cut layout carefully, so that the cut items are easy to see as they continue to detach. Using your hands, extract the negative components from around the design to expose only the design on the liner, rather than weed vinyl and iron-on.

You will appreciate that it is way simpler to weed Infusible Ink Transfer Sheets. The transition sheets are much stronger and very can be readily peeled off! Trim the liner if you needed to, so that it is not broader than the heat plate by EasyPress.

4. Step 4. To eliminate tiny dirt and fibers from the coat, use a lint roller. This may sound pointless, but do not miss it! And quite minor debris in the transfer will cause imperfections, and we obviously do not want that. Cover the shirt (which is bigger than the Easy Press heat plate) with butcher paper. In each box of Infusible Ink Transfer Sheets, Butcher paper fits in.

5. Step 5. Essential- Preheat the region where the transfer can eliminate excess liquid and wrinkles. For this task, push it for 15 seconds at 385 degrees. Allow the shirt to cool fully after removing the butcher paper.

6. Step 6. With the design faced down and the transparent liner on top, on the shirt, put the cut ink transfer design sheet. Cover with butcher paper that is broader than the heat plate from EasyPress. For 40 seconds, set the EasyPress2, then put the EasyPress at 385 degrees over the design for 40 seconds. At this moment, do not shift your hand! You want it all to be good, so the transfer does not shift at all. Raise the EasyPress 2 steadily without shaking the stack or the butcher paper as the EasyPress buzzes. Let it cool the design. Typically, the design would come straight out, but if it does not, make careful to extract it with tongs and not the fingertips. When cool, you will carefully remove that butcher paper then the filler with the design. You do not want your shirt to get destroyed!

Handmade Paper Flower Corsage

For Prom, these will also look fantastic: select colors to compliment your Prom gown and put them in a keepsake box. A (stored correctly) paper flower corsage can last for many years that can be used again. If you get the best of it, producing paper flowers is very easy.

Supplies:

- Scissors
- Ribbon or pins
- Glue
- Cardstock (in your color choice for flowers and leaves)
- Free template

Directions:

- Step 1. Print a template and split the flower template on your card stock color option.
- Step 2. Spray the paper slightly with water (it will enable you to curl the paper into the forms you want and fold that paper sheet to form shapes.
- Step 3. On each flower segment and leaves, stick the tabs together, and allow them to dry.
- Step 4. Using watercolors or labels, apply colored edges (optional). Glue together every leaf and petal to shape a flower and let it dry.
- Step 5. If you make a wrist corsage, adhere the completed flower to the ribbon after cutting its appropriate size. Position it at the back of the flower using pins for giving as a present. Wrap the corsage in a keepsake box or a cellophane bag.

Coffee Mug

It is simpler than it seems to make Cricut Coffee Mugs! This is a fun project by Cricut Explore Air that an inexperienced can build. If you think that Cricut Mugs are safe for the dishwasher, no, they're not. If you send these mugs as Christmas presents from Cricut, make sure you send a message to the receiver that these mugs only have to be hand-washed. The trouble with dishwasher cleaning is that certain dishwashers have incredibly high-temperature settings that can melt off the durable vinyl. It is safer to wash and dry with warm soapy water while you are using Cricut vinyl on the mugs.

Supplies:

1. Cricut Explore/Silhouette cutting machine
2. Permanent Vinyl
3. Transfer Tape
4. 12 x 12 Cricut Cutting Mat
5. SVG file (get it free below or use your own image)
6. Coffee Mugs

Directions:

1. Step 1. Collect supplies.
2. Step 2. Use the Silhouette or Cricut cutting machine to cut the SVG picture (or your picture), then weed the picture. Depending on the height of your mug, size the picture differently.
3. Step 3. To the weeded picture, add the transfer tape, press the image tightly on the mug while peeling back the vinyl paper.
4. Step 4. Peel the transfer tape back then you are done!

Fairy House Card

Give this card to a beloved one to rejoice, or hold it for yourselves! The card folds horizontally so that you can slide it into an envelope of 5" x 7", then pops open to expose the loveliest little fairy home! To see inside, open the little flap. The card has too many descriptions.

Supplies:

- 12" x 12" Pink cardstock
- Tape

- 12" x 12" Tan cardstock
- Glue
- 12" x 12" Brown cardstock
- Spray adhesive

Directions:
- Step 1: Uploading and Ungrouping.
- Step 2: Adjust each color's top layer to Score.
- Step 3: Choose the cut layer and score for each paint, and press attach.
- After cutting the parts, customize the front of the house as you see fit. Around the walls, the circles fall. Small accessories will go as far as they fit. Just be sure that none of the score lines are protected. To get the little parts to fit neatly towards the house's front, you can use the Spray Mount. If you are going to bring something inside the house on the walls, do that now as well.
- Step 4: Fold the house carefully along the lines of the score.
- Step 5: Put adhesive on the thin tab that sticks out of the house's back and tie this to the left side of the house. Fold it flat and allow the flattened one to dry. This means that the card folds flat and will not buckle later on.
- Step 6: Fold the tabs on the staircase piece, put adhesive on the tabs, and place them in the home from the bottom. However, you might choose to put it wherever. The key element is to guarantee that the staircase is adjacent to the front door and that the tabs are placed directly over each other, guaranteeing that the card will fold flat without an issue.
- Tip: If you are trying to hide the mouse from the back of the card in its little trap, stick it to the back of the staircase so that it is noticeable as you peek through the mouse hole.

- Adhesive the rectangular parts with some accessories, decorations, or notes you want. Rollback the tabs on the rectangle's parts, then slip it down the staircase from the bottom into the house. For a far more three-dimensional look and allow some gap between each part.
- Fold the rooftop hinge such that each tab goes from the others in the reverse direction.
- Place adhesive on the small pieces of the hinge triangle and bind them on the house roof's points. On the rear end of the roof tips, the triangle parts fall.
- Place on the roof any flowers or decorations you will need, then fold along the score line in half. Ensure the roof is folded well. To set the crease, rub your fingernail over the side.
- Attach the two tabs to the roof's hinge, then bind the roof to the tabs. To put it in order, fold the house flat and push the roof down on the tabs.
- Yeah, that is it! You have got an amazingly Fairy House Card already!

Birthday Garland Banner

Supplies

- Card stock in multiple colors
- Twine, string or ribbon
- Cricut machine and Cricut Design Space account

Directions

- Upload to Design Space the birthday cupcake SVG.
- Resize as required.
- Slice several parts into various shades.
- Remove as required from the weed and mat.
- String with twine or ribbon and showcase as desired.

Advent Calendar

Create your perfect Advent Calendar with printables and cut files that are simple to use. Customize the appearance, and in minutes, apply your shades and design. You can create one for the entire family, or you can choose to make one for all!

There are two pieces of the printable kit and other extras. This little box comes with a free PDF that can be printed or cut and use the SVG and import and cut with your Cricut to your Design Space account. The tiny numbers are also accessible as PDF and PNG to download. You should upload the PNG to Design Space and then turn the Design Cut to Print.

Supplies
1. Cardstock
2. Printer
3. Ribbon or yarn
4. Cricut machine

Directions
1. Cut and set the boxes.
2. Cut out numbers and designs and add them to one of the tiny boxes as accents.
3. Fill every box. String it up with a ribbon and make a loop with a short bow.
4. String ribbon and yarn on the wall or board.
5. Clip every box to the hanging ribbon.

CHAPTER 6: SOME WORKS YOU CAN DO WITH CRICUT EXPLORE AIR 2

Simple Projects to Start With

Custom Graphic T-shirt

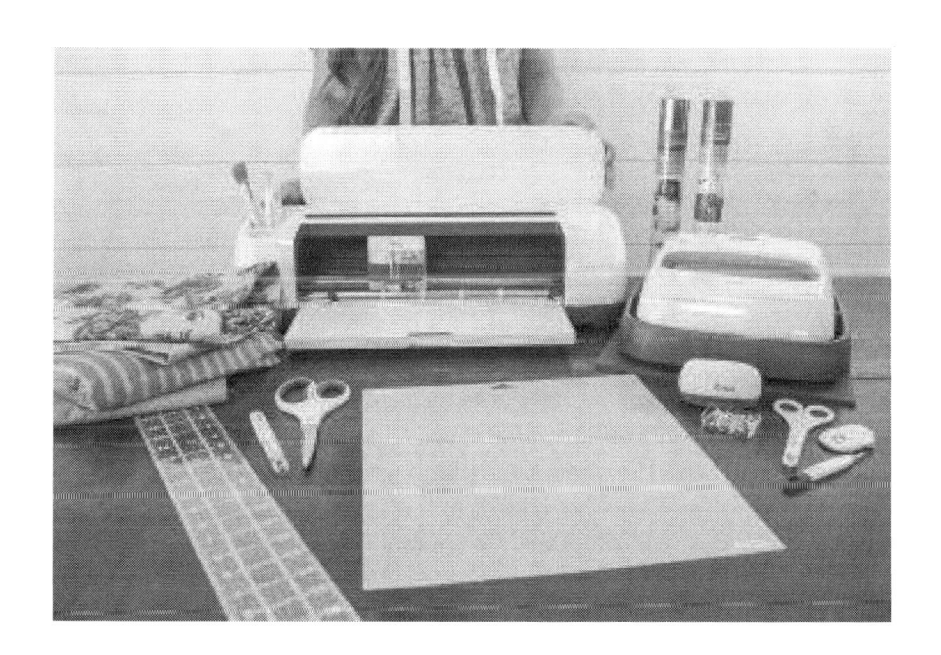

Materials
1. The Cricut Explore Air 2
2. Vinyl for the letters
3. Your Cricut tools kit

Directions

1. Start by choosing the image you want to use. This can be done in Photoshop, or you can place your text directly into the Design Space.
2. Next, open the Cricut Design Space. Choose the canvas that you wish to use by clicking the Canvas icon on the dashboard, which is located on the left-hand side. Select the canvas that you will be using for your vinyl letters. This can be anything within the categories they offer.
3. Then, select the size of the shirt for the canvas. This is located on the right-hand side of the options.
4. Now, click Upload for uploading your image, which is located on the left-hand side. Select the image you are using by browsing the list of images in your file library. Then, select the type of image that you have picked. For most projects, especially iron-on ones, you will select the Simple Cut option.
5. Click on the white space that you want to be removed by cutting out, remember to cut the insides of every letter.

1. Next, be super diligent and press Cut Image instead of Print first. You do not want to simply print the image; you cut it as well.

2. Place the image on your chosen canvas and adjust the sizing of the image.
3. Place your iron on the image with the vinyl side facing down on the mat and then turn the dial to the setting for iron on.
4. Next, you will want to click the Mirror Image setting for the image before hitting go.
5. Once you have cut the image, you should remove the excess vinyl from the edges around the lettering or image. Then use the tool for weeding out the inner pieces of the letters.
6. Now you will be placing the vinyl on the shirt.
7. And now, the fun part begins. You will get to iron the image on the shirt. Using the cotton setting, you will need to use the hottest setting that you can get your iron. There should not be any steam.
8. You want to warm the shirt by placing the iron on the shirt portion that will hold the image. This should be warmed up for 15 seconds.
9. Next, lay the vinyl out exactly where you want it to be placed. Place a pressing cloth over the top of the plastic. This will prevent the plastic on the shirt from melting.
10. Place your iron onto the pressing cloth for around 30 seconds. Flip the shirt and place the pressing cloth and iron on the back side of the vinyl.
11. Flip your shirt back over and begin to peel off the sticky part of the vinyl that you have been overlaying on the shirt. This will separate the vinyl from the plastic backing. This should be done while the plastic and vinyl are hot. If you are having trouble removing the vinyl from the plastic backing, then place the iron back on the part that is being difficult. Then proceed to pull up, and it should come off nicely.
12. This should remove the plastic from the vinyl that is now on the shirt. Place the pressing cloth on top of the vinyl once again and heat it to ensure that the vinyl is good and stuck.
13. Although there are tons of steps, it is still an amazingly simple process.

Stickers with Your Cricut

Materials

- Cricut Explore Air 2
- Printable sticker paper by Cricut

Directions

- Log in to your Cricut Design Space account.
- In the Cricut Design Space, you will need to click on Starting a New Project. Then, select the image that you would love to use for your stickers. You can use the search bar on the right-hand side at the top to locate the image that you want to use.
- Next, click on the image and click Insert Image so that the image is selected.
- Click on each one of the files that are in the image file and click the button that says Flatten at the lower right section of the screen. This will turn the individual pieces into one whole piece. This prevents the cut file from being individual pieces for the image.
- Now, you want to resize the image so that it is the size that you wish it to be. This can be any size within the recommended space for the size of the canvas.

- If you want duplicates of the image for sticker sheets, you should select all and then edit the image and click Copy. This will allow you to copy the whole row that you have selected. Once you have copied, you can then edit and paste the multiple images to make a sheet. This is the easiest way to copy and paste the image over and over again.
- At this time, you are ready to start printing your stickers. Click the Save button on the left-hand side of the screen to save the project and chose the option Save as Print and then Cut Image. Once done, you can click the green button that says Make It. This will be located in the section to the right of the screen.
- Verify that everything is how it needs to be and click Continue. This will give you a prompt to print the image onto your paper. Make sure you have used the sticker paper for the stickers. Otherwise, it won't work.
- Print out the image with your printer. If the Cricut sticker paper is too thick for your printer, using a thinner sticker paper is fine.
- After the design is printed, adjust the Smart Set dial to the appropriate setting. Place the paper onto the cutting mat and load it into the Cricut Explore Air 2 by pushing against the rollers. Press your Load and Unload button that is flashing.
- Press Go, and this will begin to cut your stickers. Since the stickers are small and intricate, you will need to be patient.
- A tip for getting a good cut is to not touch the mat and once the first cut is made and done, repress the flashing button to recut the stickers on the same lines that were previously cut.
- Now that is a great way to cut some stickers for your own needs or as a side business. Some so many people love and use stickers every day.

False Cowhide Home Keychain

Materials

- Cricut Creator
- Faux Calfskin
- Suede
- White Press On Vinyl
- Leather Paste
- Keychain Ring
- Standard Grip Tangle (green
- Iron or Simple Press

Directions

- You'll need to utilize the false cowhide for the house, the calfskin for the heart and the iron-on for "home"
- Use cowhide paste to join heart to the fluffy side of the calfskin house that doesn't show some kindness cut out.
- Put calfskin stick on the house around the heart and connect the other house, fluffy side down.
- Let sit for 30 minutes.
- Preheat the false calfskin for 35 seconds before squeezing the home on with the iron or Simple Press.
- Put the keychain ring through the entire at the highest point of the house.
- Also, in the same way, you have the ideal housewarming present for pretty much anybody!

Calfskin Hair Bow

Materials

- Cricut Investigate
- Faux Calfskin or Cowhide
- Transfer Tape
- Strong Grasp Cricut Tangle
- Bow Cricut Configuration Space Document
- E6000 Paste
- French Barrette Clasps
- Binding Clasps

Directions

- Line your artificial softened cowhide or calfskin with your exchange tape. This will give something for the texture to clutch as opposed to leaving fluff everywhere on your tangle and essentially demolishing it. This was an immense help, and I'll never return to staying the texture ideal on the solid hold tangle again.

- When you pick the artificial cowhide setting on your Keen Dial, it'll slice through the item twice. At the point when your pictures are excessively near one another, it will occasionally catch and draw the item. To stay away from this, move your pictures promote separated when you're seeing your tangle. This will spare items over the long haul and spare many cerebral pains. Try not to be hesitant to utilize some scissors if you have one knick in the calfskin.
- Begin with every one of your pieces laid out. You'll need to overlay the longest piece with the goal that the finishes compromise. Secure that with the E6000 stick and a coupling cut. On the off chance that you've made in excess of one bow, right now is an ideal opportunity to gather all the more drawn out pieces.
- Next, you'll assume the back and position some E6000 stick in the center and take your bow piece and hold it to that, safe with a coupling cut. Enable it to dry only a couple of minutes in the middle of each progression.
- Next, put some E6000 on the barrette and lay the back piece to it. Take your little center piece and apply the paste to that. Overlay it over the bow in the center and around the back of the barrette. Secure that with a coupling cut. I'd permit these to dry for a couple of hours before you stick them in their hair to make sure they don't get any paste on them.

Fun Foam Stamps

Want to work on a fun project that any kid would enjoy and that can be completed in no time? This is the perfect project for you then, as fun foam stamps are both fun to make and fun to use. You will also get a chance to make something out of craft foam sheets in combination with only a few materials and the inevitable use of your Cricut Explore Air 2. Let's see how you can make your own fun foam stamps today.

Materials
- Craft Foam Sheets

- Wooden blocks - small blocks, not larger than 4 inches
- Glue
- Cricut Explore Air 2

Directions
- Open your Design Space and go to Images. You can search for the images through the library by using specific words or browse through the library to find the images you like. You can choose letters as well if you would like to make letter stamps. Numbers can be used as well. You can use fun images of unicorns, hearts, stars, or whichever shape or image you find interesting. Use the top editing panel to size the images for your stamps. Images shouldn't be larger than 2 inches, but you can also make them larger or smaller if you prefer. Make sure to size the images to fit the wooden blocks.
- Once you click on "Make it", make sure to set the material to cutting foam as you will be using foam sheets for your designs. You can cut several images at once, while it is handy not to have more than 6 x 2-inch images prepared for cutting. Set your cutting mat and arrange your foam material – you can use different colors for different stamp images. Once you have set up everything, you can start cutting.
- Once the images are cut out, you can start gluing them to the wooden blocks. It is best to let the glue dry overnight before you start using stamps. You are all done and good to go!

CHAPTER 7: HOW YOU CAN MONETIZE FROM YOUR CREATIONS

Making Money with Cricut

Here are some questions to ask yourself before starting out. Doing an exercise like this will help you streamline your goals and ease your way forward.

Ask yourself the following questions:

- Why do you want to sell your crafts? Write down three to four reasons.
- Is this going to be something you want to do part-time, or are you considering making it become your main revenue stream?
- If it is not going to be full-time, do you have enough time to spend on crafting to sustain the business and meet customer demands?
- How well-versed are you in marketing?
- Are you capable of handling the technology side of the business?
- Where would you set up your craft workshop?
- Could you picture yourself crafting day in and day out?
- How well do you deal with difficult people?
- Are you prepared to deal with people from all walks of life?
- Do you have the support to help back you up?

These are tough questions, but a lot of small businesses fail because they weren't able to answer them ahead of time. You need to have a clear, concise plan and vision from the beginning, and you must be sure that this is what you truly want to do. Understanding the why, how, and when is the most important building block for a strong foundational base for any start-up.

There are many things you have to think about before starting your own crafting business. There are copyright issues, licensing concerns, and finding out the limitations on selling your goods, among other considerations.

Before starting out, you should find someone who is business savvy and pick their brain. What first steps do they recommend for you? What pitfalls can they help you avoid? Do the research and learn the A-Z of starting your crafting business to make sure all your I's and T's are dotted and crossed.

50+ Business Ideas You Can Make with Your Cricut and Sell

- Wall art canvas
- Leather bracelet
- Frosty wreath,
- Iron-on T-shirt
- Customized tools
- Customized cutting board
- Customized kitchen towels
- Customized lanyards
- Doormats
- Rustic signs
- Coffee mugs
- Holiday bucket
- Customized plates
- Pillows case
- Bed sheets
- Paper succulent
- Planner stickers
- Sports cuff
- Key chains

- Wooden signs
- Monogrammed ornament
- Blankets
- Laptop cases
- Monogrammed pillows
- Car stickers
- Home decals
- Christmas greeting cards
- Interior designs
- Pet tags
- Cake tops
- Scrapbook pages
- Gift boxes
- Addressed envelopes
- Felt coasters
- Customized tote bags
- Flower bouquets
- Monogrammed water bottle
- Model decals
- Paper pennants
- Metallic tags
- Paper peonies
- Santa sacks
- Christmas advent calendar
- Paper heart box
- Paper tulips
- Magnolia blossom
- Gift card holder

- Paper flower lanterns
- Paper purse
- Paper poppers
- Halloween buddies
- Paper fiery house and more

Ideas for Selling Your Cricut Crafts

The following ideas assume that you have the full legal rights to sell all the crafts you are making.

- First, narrow down your product niche. Find a few products that you enjoy creating and that there is a demand for.
- Be creative and unique. Make your own niche or start a new trend. You want there to be a market for your product, but not one that's already oversaturated.
- Don't shy away from festivals or markets. Find out when and where there are events in or around your area. Get yourself out there. Ask your friends and family to come with you.
- Make flyers! Yes, people do still use flyers, especially at large events. You need to draw people's attention to you. Flyers can be annoying, but they also get a person's attention.
- Give small samples of your products out. If people like them, they'll be encouraged to come back for more, this time with their wallets ready.
- Ask family and friends to use your products. There is no quicker way to catch a person's eye than when someone else has something they don't or is using it regularly. Family and friends are great promoters, and since they are by your side, they can be your staunchest supporters. They can also give you positive reviews and testimonials online.

- Build a website. There are many easy-to-use websites such as Wix, Squarespace, Moonfruit, and more. They have hundreds of already-made templates that you can easily customize to suit your needs. You can even start a crafting blog with tips, tricks, and project instructions to pull more people in.
- Use social media to your advantage. Facebook, Twitter, Instagram, and all the other social media platforms out there can help get your products seen by potentially millions of customers.
- There is no harm in approaching small shops that sell arts and crafts to ask them to take some consignment stock.
- Make your gifts for baby showers, birthdays, holidays, and even weddings.
- You can rent small stalls in large shopping malls. These stalls are usually in the middle of busy walkways.

These are some of the ways to get your crafts out there and make money selling customized homemade goods. What you have to remember when you do start selling your crafts is that it may not take off right away. Most of the successful businesses out there today had slow or rocky starts. You can't give up on your first try. If you are serious about making money with your crafts, you have to push through the hard times to get to the good ones.

Online Marketplaces for Selling Crafts

The websites that you will find below are probably already familiar to you, even by hearsay, because they are the most popular in the craft world. All allow you to create your store within it, with your name, logo, and description; display your items, serve your customers, and manage orders and payments. So they work in much the same way. As I anticipated, Etsy is the most famous globally, and especially in the United States. DaWanda stands out particularly in Europe, with a large influx of German public. I will tell you in a little more detail.

Etsy

Etsy is an American platform that has been growing in popularity since it was created to become the number 1 marketplace to sell handmade worldwide. Here you can sell all kinds of handmade products, as well as vintage and even DIY materials and patterns. Besides, you can find forums and discussion groups with a lot of activities in which to connect with like-minded people. Most are in English. Fortunately, not all. Due to the huge volume of traffic that this platform has every day, especially from the United States, it is one of the marketplaces preferred by many artisans to start. Opening a store is easier than it may seem a priori, especially if you follow some tutorial that explains step by step and in great detail how you can open your store on Etsy.

Creating your own shop on Etsy will cost you nothing. What you will have to pay is a publication fee of 20 cents for each item you put up for sale in your store, in addition to a 3.5% commission for each transaction.

Artesanum

The world's arts and crafts store Artesanum is a platform that was created to become the largest online market for the sale of arts and crafts in Spanish. Something that I value very positively is that it was founded in 2007 as a social project of the Intercom Group, and it donates the profits generated by Artesanum to projects related to crafts. Also, artisans agree that it is very easy to use. Something that differentiates it from other marketplaces is that purchases are made directly from the artisan, so the customer buys and pays at each Artesanum store independently (this means that they do not collect items from different stores in a cart).

Who creates a store in Artesanum has two possibilities:

- Use your store as a showcase to list your crafts and contact potential buyers by courier for free.
- Add payment tools to the store in exchange for 5% for each sale.

As I mentioned at the beginning, my intention with this compilation is to offer you a lot of possibilities to sell your crafts online with little investment so that you can choose the ones that suit you best. That bunch of options certainly includes more marketplaces. The online marketplaces below may not be that popular, but... who knows. Perhaps among them, you discover the perfect option for you.

Lulìshop

I had the opportunity to chat with the team that created this marketplace to tell me more about the project and have already published the interview on the blog. If you have not seen it and you do not know anything about this marketplace, I can tell you that it was created in Corsica with the idea of facilitating the online sale of their crafts to artisans in that region and due to the success achieved it has been extended to focus on the sale of Mediterranean crafts today.

Coolmaison

Coolmaison is an online craft store specializing in handmade jewelry, tableware, and decoration, which stands out for its designs' exclusivity and quality. It is a platform that is committed to avant-garde craftsmanship, so not just any handmade piece is worth being there. Artisans who want to sell with them must send their application and go through a selection process.

Once inside, you will have a dashboard where you can find all the information, promotional tools, and statistics. When you have orders and messages from clients, they will inform you by e-mail. If you are targeting an audience that buys designer handmade, Coolmaison could be the perfect option for you.

Unique Species

Unique Species is an online store that sells handmade items that are characterized by their design, uniqueness, and sustainability. This makes them very selective with the products that are sold since they seek to guarantee their customers their quality and sustainability.

They are in charge of all the management and promotion of the items in the store. You will only have to worry about sending the order when they contact you to communicate that there has been a sale. Like other platforms of the style, it works on commission. And they are open to working with new professionals like you If you think that your creations could fit into that concept of "unique species" and you want to become one of the partners of this online store, go ahead and contact them.

CHAPTER 8: FREQUENTLY ASKED QUESTIONS

This section will address the most common issues with the Cricut experience, as well as some of the most common questions that come up. If there is an answer you can't find here, the internet is an exceptionally useful tool when it comes to troubleshooting or just understanding your Cricut system.

Why is My Material Tearing?

The two most common causes for this unfortunate problem are dull blades or blades that have a buildup of residue on them.

Do I Need to Convert My Image to an SVG?

It is not necessary to convert your images to the SVG format if you have a JPG or PNG. However, if you wish to convert your files, there are several free online resources that can help you with this process. Do bear in mind that if you convert your file type to an SVG, you may have less freedom to manipulate the components of your image.

Where Can I Buy Materials?

Materials for the Cricut to cut can be found at a nearly limitless number of places. Since the Cricut is such a versatile machine with the ability to cut so many materials, you won't be able to go into any crafting or fabric stores without tripping over new materials you can use for your latest and greatest crafts.

As you continue to explore the world of Cricut, you'll get a feel for which materials and which brands best suit your needs. From there, shopping online to find the best price for those materials and brands can help you to make your dollar go as far as it can go!

Do I Need a Printer to Use My Cricut?

In short, no, you don't! Your Cricut comes ready to cut materials out of your materials, right out of the box. There are materials on which you can print images that you like, which you can then cut with your Cricut machine. This is known as the Print Then Cut method, and it's very popular for things like iron-on decals, stickers, temporary tattoos, and more!

Where Can I Get Compatible Images?

Thanks to the ability of Design Space to make use of so many different file types, it can be difficult to find an image that isn't compatible with your Design Space! Anywhere you can find images, you can find ones to use with your Cricut system. It is important to mind copyrights and restrictions on usage for images that you find. If you're making something that you intend to sell, you will need to make sure the image you have is licensed for reproduction and resale!

Where Can I Get Compatible Fonts?

The internet has a lot of great resources for fonts, and one of the many great things about Design Space is that all the fonts you have installed on your computer are available for use in the Design Space under "System Fonts." The thing to bear in mind is, like with images, fonts are copyrighted, and you will need to make sure that the font you have is licensed for your intended uses before you commit to one!

Why is My Blade Cutting All the Way through My Material?

This can be due to the blade being seated in the housing improperly and can also be due to an incorrect material setting on your Cricut. Always be sure to set the dial on the right of your machine for the material you're using.

Do I Need to Be Connected to the Internet to Use Design Space?

Cricut's Design Space application is entirely cloud-based. This means that you do need an active, high-speed internet connection in order to make use of the application. However, this cloud functionality enables you to access your account and your projects from any device, in any location that has a high-speed internet connection!

Which Operating Systems Are Compatible with Design Space?

Cricut Design Space is currently compatible with devices operating in the latest systems for Windows, Mac, Android, and iOS. If you have questions about your device's compatibility with the latest plugin for Cricut's Design Space, simply visit their page on system requirements and see what is listed there for you and the operating system you use.

Can I Use Design Space on My Chromebook?

Cricut's Design Space isn't currently optimized for compatibility with the Chromebook operating system. The need to download the plugin for the application is a current barrier for that operating system, but this isn't to say there is no possibility for compatibility in the near future.

Can I Use Design Space on Multiple Devices I Own?

Yes! Thanks to Design Space being entirely cloud-based, you can access your account, your projects, your designs, fonts, purchases, and images from any compatible device with an active internet connection! Design projects on your mobile device while on the go and wrap them up when you're back at home. Start a design before work and tweak it on your lunch break. The possibilities are limitless, and now so is Design Space.

Is There a Time Limit on Using Images I've Purchased through Design Space?

Images, fonts, and projects purchased through Cricut's Design Space are yours to own and use forever. There is no time limit or expiration date for usage, and there is no limit to the number of times or ways in which you can use what you've purchased. Once you purchase an item, it is yours in every sense!

How Can I Unweld an Image in Design Space?

Unfortunately, there is no unweld option currently available in Design Space. If you weld an image, however, you can still click "Undo" if you have not saved the changes to your project. It is recommended that you save your images locally at each different stage, so you have clean images to work with for every project.

How Do I Set Design Space to Operate on the Metric System?

On your computer (this is true for both Windows and Mac), click the three stacked lines in the upper left-hand corner. From there, click Settings. In those settings, you'll see the option to set inches or centimeters as the default measurement.

If you're using Design Space on your mobile device, you will access your settings from the bottom of your screen. You may need to scroll or swipe to the left to view all your options, but this setting is available on mobile as well!

What Types of Images Can I Upload through Cricut's Design Space iOS or Android Apps?

You can currently upload any images that are saved in the Photos or Gallery app on your Apple or Android device! If you have SVG files saved, you can upload those as well. It is important to note, however, that Design Space does not support the .TIFF or .PDF files of any size. Be sure that what you're uploading is of a compatible format before uploading. Changes made on the mat do not affect your canvas!

Using Move and Hide, Can I Move Printable Images to Another Mat?

At this time, printable images cannot be moved to another mat.

In Move and Hide, Is it Possible to Move Multiple Images to a New Mat All at Once?

Currently this feature is only available on mobile iOS devices. Selecting an image, tapping and holding on other images to select them as well, multiple images can be moved at once. There is no indication as to whether this will change in the future.

How Many Images Can I Move to One Mat?

There is not currently a limit to the number of images you can put onto a mat. If they fit, you're all clear!

Can I Save Money by Hiding Images from the Mat?

The price of a project does not update to reflect whether or not images have been hidden. If the image has been included in the design in any capacity, you will incur the charge for that element.

Can I Save the Layout of My Mat?

Mat layouts cannot currently be saved. When you return to your canvas, the changes made to all your mats will be reset.

Is Cricut Design Space Compatible with My Version of Internet Explorer?

Microsoft has begun to phase out Internet Explorer. As such, it is not up to date or able to keep up with the components of Cricut Design Space. Check the Cricut website for the most up-to-date information on system and browser requirements. At the time of writing, however, the latest versions of the following browsers are compatible with Cricut Design Space.

- Apple Safari
- Google Chrome
- Microsoft Edge
- Mozilla Firefox

If you are switching over to one of these browsers from Internet Explorer, take the time to familiarize yourself with it, get your bookmarks and favorites imported, and then visit design.cricut.com to download the plugin. From here, setup with your machine will be a breeze, and you'll be off and crafting in no time!

What Features Are Available on Which Apps?

Here is a handy chart that lays out exactly what features are available in the Cricut Design Space, as well as what platforms support each feature! Be sure to consult this chart if you're weighing the options of which platform to get for your crafting experience.

Feature	Windows/Mac	iOS App	Android App
3D layer visualization		/	
Attach	/	/	/
Bluetooth compatible	/	/	/
Contour	/	/	/
Curve Text	/		

Cut & write in one step	/	/	/
Flatten to print	/	/	/
Image upload	/	/	/
Knife Blade cutting	/		
Link Physical Cartridges	/		
Machine setup	/	/	/
Offline		/	
Pattern fills	/		
Photo Canvas		/	
Print then cut	/	/	
Slice and weld	/	/	/
Smart Guides		/	/
SnapMat		/	
System fonts	/	/	/
Templates	/		
Writing style fonts	/	/	/

CHAPTER 9: TIPS & STRATEGIES FOR THE FIRST PROJECT

So, you've got all of your supplies on hand, which is great, but how are you using the Cricut machine? Yeah, that is what you are going to find out about. If gazing at your Cricut machine leaves you feeling puzzled, then keep on reading; we're going to teach you how to use your latest Cricut machine in an easy but productive way.

Setting the Machine

Next, you'll want to set up a machine for Cricut. To start, build a space for it. The perfect place for it is a craft room, but if you are at a loss about where to place it if necessary, we consider setting it up in a dining room. Be certain you get an outlet near or a secure extension cord. Learn the directions next. You can hop straight in and start using the devices, but it can be very boring with Cricut machines. The easiest thing to do is read all the materials you receive for your machine - while we're going to go over the setup in this book, have a peek at the manual if you're still perplexed.

Please ensure you have enough free space around the unit itself since you're going to load mats in and out, and you're going to need that little bit of wiggle room. Of course, the machine where the drawings can be made is the next thing to set up. Be sure that there is an internet link with the medium you are using, as you will need to install the Cricut Design Space software. It would need to be plugged in directly if it's a laptop older than the Explore Air 2, so if it's a wireless machine like the Air 2, you can easily add it to your phone, and then from there, configure what you need to design. You'll like to learn how to use Design Space once you get this bad boy originally set up, and this is what we'll talk about next.

Using Tools from Cricut

So, Cricut machines use a software called Cricut Design Spaces; when you're finished, you'll have to ensure you have it downloaded and enabled. If you are going to use a smartphone or tablet or if you're on a device, download the app and go to http://design.cricut.com/setup to get the apps. Make sure that you have Bluetooth connectivity allowed on the system or the cable is plugged in if it is not already connected up. Keep the power button in order to turn the computer on. You'll then head to the settings to display your Cricut model in the Bluetooth configuration. Choose it, and your computer will ask you to put in a Bluetooth passcode from there. Only find this something easy to recall and generic.

You will now use the Design Room until that's completed. So, what I love about Design Space is that it's amazingly convenient to use. They know that you're a novice, so you'll find that navigation is really fast. We want to use the Design Space app, as this would allow you to upload any design to the cloud so that your designs can be reused. Even so, if you're using them without getting an internet connection, instead of depending on the cloud, you'll want to make sure that you save it and save it to the system itself.

You can see a lot of projects you can use while you are in the online mode. We recommend making sure you bring a simple one for the sake of this guide, such as the "Enjoy Card" project that you'll get instantly. Then you've all connected to everything-move. Let's on to the first cut for this project.

Cartridges and Keypad

The first cut you're going to make includes the feedback of the keyboard and cartridges, and both are generally done for the project "Enjoy Card" that you will get straight away. So, pick this project after it is set up, and then from there, you can now use the tools and accessories inside the project. Until you get to do your tasks, you may need to configure the smart dial.

It's on the right-hand side of Explore Air 2, and it's the way you pick your materials, essentially. Turn the dial to what kind of material you choose, as this helps to ensure that you have the proper blade adjustments. There are also half of the configurations for those projects in between.

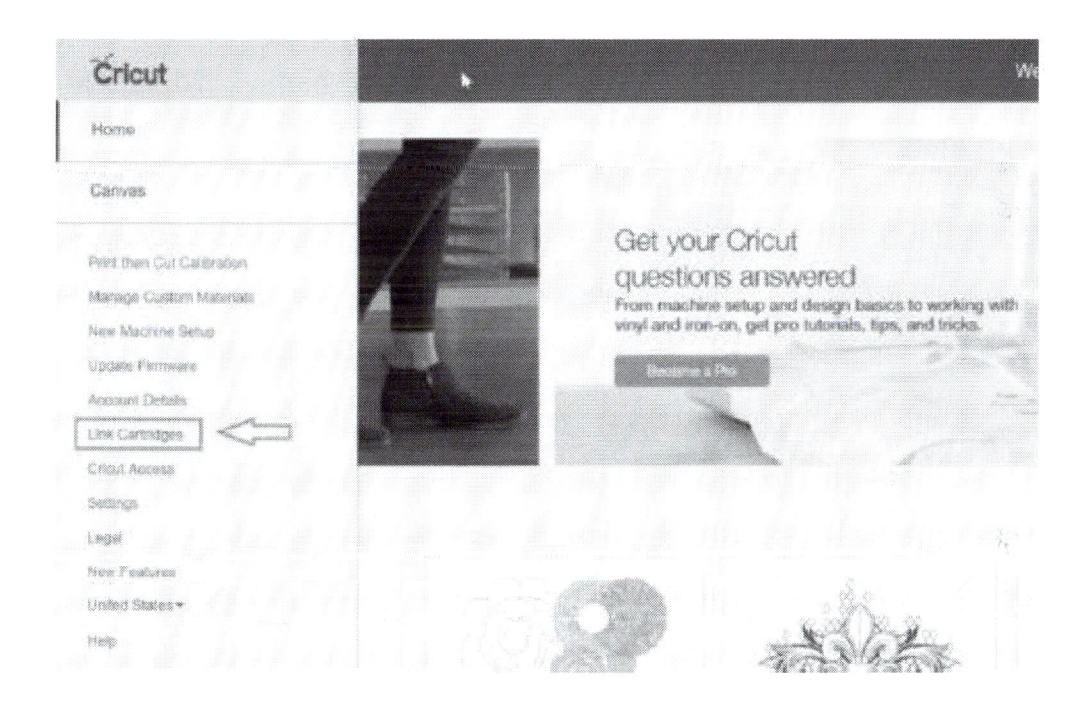

Let us just say, for starters, you've got some light cardstock. The setting, or the corresponding half setting, may be preferred. Your machine will automatically adapt to the right setting until this is selected in Design Space. You can also select the quick mode on the screen in the 'set, load, go' area, so you can then verify the box's location under the dial position indicator. Click this then, and cut. The fast mode, though, is extremely loud, so be careful. We have listed cartridges now. Although these are typically no longer used in the Explore Air 2 units, they help start-up projects. "To do this, go to the hamburger menu until you have the Design Space app, and everything is connected, and you'll see an alternative called "ink cartridges." Click that bad boy, and pick the Cricut system from there. You would then be instructed by the computer to bring the cartridge in. Do it, and it will instruct you to attach the cartridge until it's identified.

Please note, however, that you can't use it with other devices until you mount this the one restriction on these cartridges. You can go to the photos until it's official and select the cartridge option to find the ones you want to make. To find out what you need, you can sort the cartridges, and you can search out your photos tab for any other cartridges that are bought or posted. Digital cartridges can be purchased, which means you purchase them digitally and select the photos directly from the options available. They aren't real, so no connecting is possible.

Paper loading and unloading

You'll like to ensure the paper is at minimum three inches by three inches to load paper into the Cricut system. It won't cut too well anyway. For this, you can use daily files. Now you'll have to position the paper on the cutting mat to make this work. You are One of the ones you ought to have, so say it straight now and remove the attached movie. Place a paper corner in the area where you are guided to match the corners of the paper. From there, transfer the paper for proper adherence straight onto the cutting pad. When you do so, you just load it using the arrows into the computer. You're going to want to keep the document on the mat tightly. Click the key to the "load paper" you see when you do this. When for whatever reason, it doesn't take, Click the paper key to unload it, then begin again before it emerges.

Currently, you can still have a prototype cut in order before you do some cutting for your template. Some don't do this, so when studying how to use a Cricut, it's incredibly beneficial. Otherwise, in some situations, you won't get the pressure right, so get in the habit of doing it with your bits. Is there really a disparity between other items and vinyl? The main slicing mats are different. You may need to have a grip, or lack thereof, based on what you're slicing. If you think like the material does not really stick properly, have some Heat N 'Bond to assist with this because the trouble with cutting materials always stems from the fact that it doesn't stick. And to help have a better grip on these, you may also need mats that are a bit tougher as well.

How to detach your cut from the cutting mat?

It's simple but difficult to remove the cut from the mat. Individually, because they love to just hang around there, we fell into the dilemma of things getting more difficult for vinyl designs. And we'll clarify how you can make and eliminate nice cuts, as well.

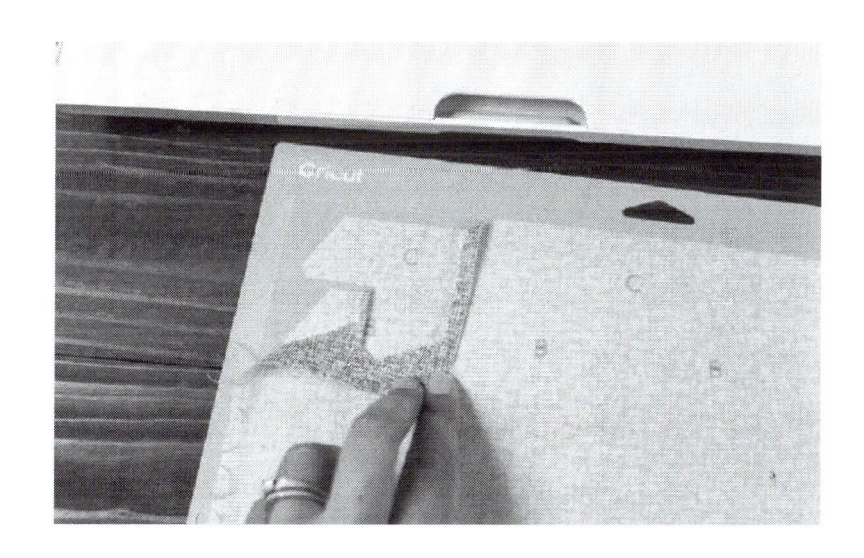

The first thing to consider is to make sure the right mat is used by you. For very light stuff, the light grip ones are fantastic, with the pink one being among the best, and only to be used on the Cricut Builder. You would undoubtedly be eager for Cleaver to remove the project immediately from the mat after the plan is cut, but one of the issues with this is that sometimes, and if you're not cautious, the project will be lost. Bend the mat in your palm, rather than taking the project from of the mat itself but force it away from the project, as this would release it from the mat. Bend this both horizontally and vertically until the project is freed by the adhesive.

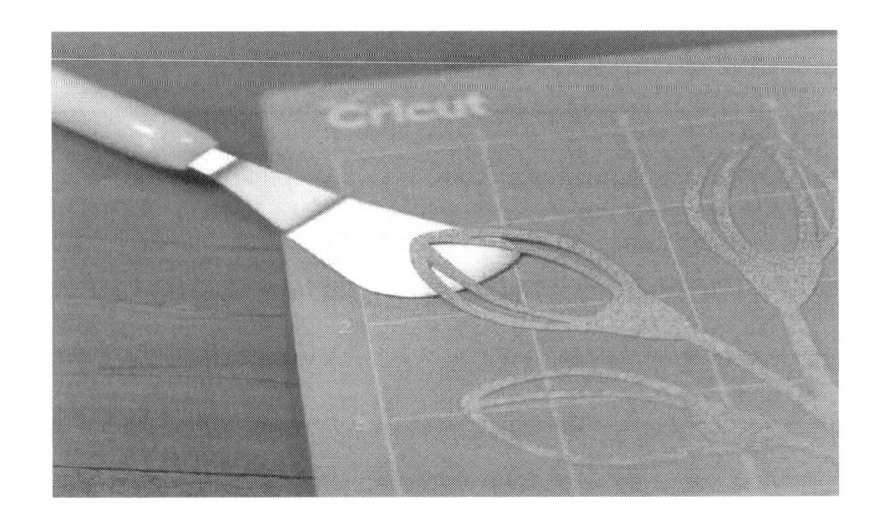

Do you recall the spatula instrument we advised you to get early on with your Cricut machine? This is where it is used for you. To tug on the vinyl gently, use this spatula so you can take it from the corner and pick it up. You risk curling it otherwise or tearing the mat, which is what we don't want.

Now, this would be unbelievably simple with the original cuts, such as the paper ones. We were shocked by how little work it took, but one of the best attempts; things to keep in mind are that when extracting the stuff, you have to go slow with Cricut machines. Do the same grade, and at the end, don't panic. Taking your time and you'll save a lot of hassle, and it'll also save you cash and also save you anxiety! You'll find that the Cricut mats are extremely sticky, and metal spatulas will function as well if you're not using a Cricut spatula on hand or don't need to spend money. The paper should be placed on a smooth surface and then pulled gently.

However, when you remove these objects, always be patient. Cricut machines are fairly easy to use, and the advantage is that you really can make any things you like with the correct view and ideas.

CHAPTER 10: CRICUT EXPLORE AIR 2 PROJECT IDEAS WITH VINYL

Trick or Treat Bag

Materials needed – "Cricut Maker" or "Cricut Explore", standard grip mat, transfer tape, scraper, everyday vinyl, small craft paper bags.

Step 1

Log into the "Design Space" application and click on the "New Project" button on the top right corner of the screen to view a blank canvas.

Step 2

Click on the "Images" icon and type in "Halloween" in the search bar, then click on "Insert Images" at the bottom of the screen. The image selected is shown in the picture below.

Step 3

You can edit either or both the image as needed by clicking on applicable tools on the "Edit Bar".

Step 4

Select the entire design and click on the "Group" icon. Then click on "Save" to save the project.

Step 5

Simply click on the "Make It" button and load the vinyl sheet to your "Cricut" machine and follow the instructions on the screen to cut your project.

Step 6

Carefully remove the excess vinyl from the sheet. To easily paste your design on the craft bag without stretching the pieces, put the transfer tape on top of the cut design. Now, slowly peel the paper backing on the vinyl from one end to the other in a rolling motion to ensure even placement and use the scraper tool on top of the transfer tape to remove any bubbles and then just peel off the transfer tape.

Personalized Mugs (Iron-On Vinyl)

Materials needed – "Cricut Maker" or "Cricut Explore", standard grip mat, printable "Cricut" iron-on or heat transfer vinyl, "Cricut Easy Press Mini", "Easy Press" mat, weeding tool, ceramic mug.

Step 1

Log into the "Design Space" application and click on the "New Project" button on the top right corner of the screen to view a blank canvas.

Step 2

Click on the "Images" icon on the "Design Panel" and type in "America" in the search bar. Click on the desired image, then click on the "Insert Images" button at the bottom of the screen.

Step 3

Click on the "Templates" icon on the "Designs Panel" on the left of the screen and type in "mug" in the templates search bar, and select the mug icon.

Step 4

You can change the "Type" and "Size" of the template to decorate mugs with non-standard sizes by clicking on the "Size" icon and selecting "Custom" to update your mug size.

Step 5

You can further edit your design by clicking on the "Shapes" icon, adding hearts, stars or other desired shapes to your design.

Step 6

Click on "Save" at the top right corner of the screen and give the desired name to the project, for example, "Mug Decoration" and click "Save".

Step 7

The design is ready to be printed and cut. Simply click on the "Make It" button and follow the prompts on the screen for using the inkjet printer to print the design on your printable iron-on vinyl and subsequently cut the design.

Step 8

Carefully remove the excess material from the sheet using the "weeder tool", making sure only the design remains on the clear liner.

Step 9

Using the "Cricut Easy Press Mini" and "Easy Press Mat" the iron-on layers can be easily transferred to your mug. Preheat your "Easy Press Mini" and put your design on the desired area and apply pressure for a couple of minutes or more (Sample project in the picture below). Wait for few minutes prior to peeling off the design while it is still warm. (Since the design is delicate, use the spatula tool or your fingers to rub the letters down the mug before starting to peel the design)

Personalized Coaster Tiles

Materials needed – "Cricut Maker" or "Cricut Explore", standard grip mat, printable "Cricut" iron-on or heat transfer vinyl, "Cricut Easy Press Mini", "Easy Press" mat, weeding tool, ceramic coaster tiles.

Step 1

Log into the "Design Space" application and click on the "New Project" button on the top right corner of the screen to view a blank canvas.

Step 2

Let's use our own image for this project. Search the web to find a monogram image that you would like and store it on your computer. Now, click on the "Upload" icon from the "Designer Panel" on the left of the screen.

Step 3

A screen with "Upload Image" and "Upload Pattern" will be displayed. Click on the "Upload Image" button. Click on "Browse" or simply drag and drop your image on the screen. Select the image type "Simple" and save the image as a "Print Then Cut image".

Step 4

Choose the uploaded image by clicking on the "Insert Images" and edit the image as needed. You can personalize the monogram by adding text to the design by clicking on the "Text" icon and typing in "Your Name" or any other phrase.

Step 5

For the image below, the font "American Uncial Corn Regular" in Regular and color (green) were selected. Select the text and the image and click on "Group", then copy-paste your design as many times as needed and save the project.

Step 6

You can resize the design as needed to match the size of your coaster, although the recommended size is 4 x 4 inches for most common tile coasters. The design is ready to be printed and cut. Simply click on the "Make It" button and follow the prompts on the screen for using the inkjet printer to print the design on your printable iron-on vinyl and subsequently cut the design.

Step 7

Carefully remove the excess material from the sheet using the "weeder tool", making sure only the design remains on the clear liner.

Step 8

Using the "Cricut Easy Press Mini" and "Easy Press Mat" the iron-on layers can be easily transferred to your mug. Preheat your "Easy Press Mini" and put your design on the desired area and apply pressure for a couple of minutes or more. Wait for few minutes prior to peeling off the design while it is still warm.

Vinyl Chalkboard

Materials needed – "Cricut Maker" or "Cricut Explore", standardgrip mat, Cricut Linen vinyl in desired colors, weeder, transfer tape, chalkboard, and chalk pen.

Step 1

Log into the "Design Space" application and click on the "New Project" button on the top right corner of the screen to view a blank canvas.

Step 2

Click on the "Projects" icon and type in "vinyl chalkboard" in the search bar.

Step 3

Click on "Customize" to further edit the project to your preference, or simply click on the "Make It" button and load the vinyl sheet to your "Cricut" machine and follow the instructions on the screen to cut your project.

Step 4

Using a weeder tool, remove the negative space pieces of the design. Use the transfer tape to apply the vinyl cuts to the chalkboard. Then use the scraper tool on top of the transfer tape to remove any bubbles and then just peel off the transfer tape. Lastly, use a chalk pen to write messages.

Vinyl Herringbone Bracelet

Materials needed – "Cricut Maker" or "Cricut Explore", standardgrip mat, vinyl (midnight), weeder, scraper, transfer tape, metal bracelet gold.

Step 1
Log into the "Design Space" application and click on the "New Project" button on the top right corner of the screen to view a blank canvas.

Step 2
Click on the "Images" icon on the "Design Panel" and type in "#M33278" in the search bar. Select the image and click on the "Insert Images" button at the bottom of the screen.

Step 3
Click on "Customize" to further edit the project to your preference, or simply click on the "Make It" button and load the vinyl sheet to your "Cricut" machine and follow the instructions on the screen to cut your project.

Step 4
Using a weeder tool, remove the negative space pieces of the design. Use the transfer tape to apply the vinyl cuts to the bracelet. Then use the scraper tool on top of the transfer tape to remove any bubbles and then just peel off the transfer tape.

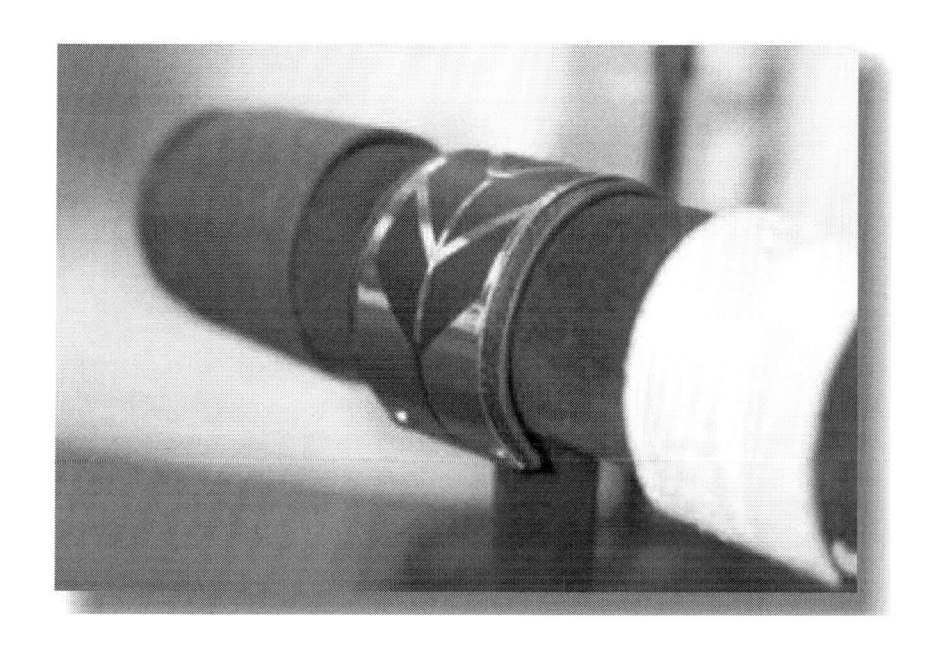

Cloud Vinyl Wallpaper

Materials needed – "Cricut Maker" or "Cricut Explore", standardgrip mat, vinyl (midnight), weeder, scraper, transfer tape, metal bracelet gold.

Step 1
Log into the "Design Space" application and click on the "New Project" button on the top right corner of the screen to view a blank canvas.

Step 2
Click on the "Images" icon on the "Design Panel" and type in "#M4C5D3" in the search bar. Select the image and click on the "Insert Images" button at the bottom of the screen.

Step 3
Edit the project to your preference, or simply click on the "Make It" button and load the vinyl sheet to your "Cricut" machine and follow the instructions on the screen to cut your project.

Step 4

Using a weeder tool, remove the negative space pieces of the design. Use the transfer tape to apply the vinyl cuts to the wall in a wallpaper like pattern. Then use the scraper tool on top of the transfer tape to remove any bubbles and then just peel off the transfer tape.

Printable Vinyl Easter Eggs

Materials needed – "Cricut Maker" or "Cricut Explore", standardgrip mat, printable vinyl, weeder, transfer tape, scraper, home printer, hard boiled eggs, Easter egg dye.

Step 1

Log into the "Design Space" application and click on the "New Project" button on the top right corner of the screen to view a blank canvas.

Step 2

Click on the "Projects" icon and type in "vinyl Easter eggs" in the search bar.

Step 3

Click on "Customize" to further edit the project to your preference, or simply click on the "Make It" button and load the vinyl sheet to your "Cricut" machine and follow the instructions on the screen to cut your project.

Step 4

The design is ready to be printed and cut. Simply click on the "Make It" button and follow the prompts on the screen for using the inkjet printer to print the design on your printable vinyl and subsequently cut the design.

Step 5

Carefully remove the excess material from the sheet using the "weeder tool", making sure only the design remains on the clear liner.

Step 6

Using the dye paint and the hard boiled eggs. Then use the transfer tape to apply the vinyl cuts to the eggs. Then use the scraper tool on top of the transfer tape to remove any bubbles and then just peel off the transfer tape.

Game over Tablet Vinyl

Materials needed – "Cricut Maker" or "Cricut Explore", standardgrip mat, vinyl (midnight), weeder, scraper, transfer tape, tablet.

Step 1
Log into the "Design Space" application and click on the "New Project" button on the top right corner of the screen to view a blank canvas.

Step 2
Click on the "Projects" icon and type in "table vinyl" in the search bar.

Step 3
Simply click on the "Make It" button and load the vinyl sheet to your "Cricut" machine and follow the instructions on the screen to cut your project.

Step 4
Using a weeder tool, remove the negative space pieces of the design. Use the transfer tape to apply the vinyl cuts to the tablet. Then use the scraper tool on top of the transfer tape to remove any bubbles and then just peel off the transfer tape.

CONCLUSION

Thank you for making it to the end. The Cricut Explore Air 2 is an affordable home cutting machine that makes it easy to create photo-realistic images, as well as other designs. Unlike the original Explore Air, this model can cut materials like fabric and leather. The Explore Air 2 also features a smaller cutting area, measuring 12" x 12", which is larger than most home machines but not large enough for several projects at once. It's not the best solution for customers who expect to cut frequently or have a lot of projects planned; instead, it makes sense for someone who needs a cutting system occasionally or wants to use it only for detailed work.

The Cricut Explore Air 2 costs $229 on its own or $299 if you want the cartridge package deal. However, you can find discounts online that lower this price by about $30 to $40. You should also be able to save money by purchasing your machine through Amazon rather than directly from Cricut (where prices tend to be higher). For example, Amazon's Explore Air 2 with the Cricut Explore Air 2 starter kit sells for $239.95, while a similar machine sold directly from the Cricut brand by itself would cost over $299.

This is a home device, so it's not designed to cut materials that would be damaged with high-speed motors. Most customers will use it to create images or designs that they can print onto fabric or paper for calendars and gifts. It also makes an excellent alternative to traditional presses and canvas (for example, for creating invitations, photos, and prints), especially when you want to make many copies of your designs. This model cuts "through" materials like paper and fabric rather than "on" them; this reduces wear on your cutting mat. Also keep in mind that this machine is not equipped with a plastic blade guard; although you can always cover the blade to protect it from damage during use, there's no safety feature built-in that will automatically stop your work if something jams in the machine along the way (for example, if you're cutting through thick cardstock).

The Explore Air 2 is designed for people who use cutting machines occasionally or want a system for personal projects. The plug-and-play operation means that you can quickly set it up, create a design, and cut materials without having to spend time on computer programs or downloading images. It also has an easy-to-use software package; while more advanced users will appreciate the control, it's not complicated enough to be intimidating. As long as you're willing to stick to included designs and don't expect sophisticated features (like font options), the machine is easy enough for novice users or younger children. This model should also please customers who have been frustrated by the high cost or limited capabilities of other home cutting machines; the Explore Air 2 offers more options than some competitors at a lower price point. It's also portable with an included carrying case and can create up to 1,000 designs on its own or store up to 4,000 images in its flash storage (without an SD card). The cutter can cut several different materials, including paper, cardstock, vinyl banners, fabric strips, leathers and more. It's compatible with a variety of cartridges, including Cricut Elements, Cricut Craft Room and Cricut Maker.

The Explore Air 2 is designed as an affordable alternative to heavier professional cutting machines like those made by Silhouette and Xyron; however, it offers less capability than some competitors (for example, you won't find any features related to embossing). It also lacks some capabilities that are found in larger models like the Silhouette Design Studio: there are no vinyl cutter or laminator options available.

I hope you have learned something!

Manufactured by Amazon.ca
Bolton, ON